The Everyday Chef

BAKERY

COOKING

Celebrity Press • Nashville, Tennessee

Text copyright © 1997 by Hambleton-Hill Publishing, Inc.
Some or all of the photographic images in this book were provided by
Digital Stock, Corporation
1-800-545-4514

Published by Celebrity Press
An imprint of Hambleton-Hill Publishing, Inc.
Nashville, Tennessee 37218

Printed and bound in the United States of America

ISBN 1-58029-018-3

10 9 8 7 6 5 4 3 2 1

Graphic Design/Art Direction
John Laughlin

Contents

Conversion Table

Metric Conversions

1/8 teaspoon = .05 ml
1/4 teaspoon = 1 ml
1/2 teaspoon = 2 ml
1 teaspoon = 5 ml
1 tablespoon = 3 teaspoons = 15 ml
1/8 cup = 1 fluid ounce = 30 ml
1/4 cup = 2 fluid ounces = 60 ml
1/3 cup = 3 fluid ounces = 90 ml
1/2 cup = 4 fluid ounces = 120 ml
2/3 cup = 5 fluid ounces = 150 ml

3/4 cup = 6 fluid ounces = 180 ml
1 cup = 8 fluid ounces = 240 ml
2 cups = 1 pint = 480 ml
2 pints = 1 liter
1 quart = 1 liter
1/2 inch = 1.25 centimeters
1 inch = 2.5 centimeters
1 ounce = 30 grams
1 pound = 0.5 kilogram

Oven Temperatures

Fahrenheit	Celsius
250°F	120°C
275°F	140°C
300°F	150°C
325°F	160°C
350°F	180°C
375°F	190°C
400°F	200°C
425°F	220°C
450°F	230°C

Baking Dish Sizes

American	Metric
8-inch round baking dish	20-centimeter dish
9-inch round baking dish	23-centimeter dish
11 x 7 x 2-inch baking dish	28 x 18 x 4-centimeter dish
12 x 8 x 2-inch baking dish	30 x 19 x 5-centimeter dish
9 x 5 x 3-inch baking dish	23 x 13 x 6-centimeter dish
1 1/2-quart casserole	1.5-liter casserole
2-quart casserole	2-liter casserole

Muffins

Batter:

A thin mixture of flour and liquid that is combined with other ingredients to make foods such as cakes.

Beat:

To mix ingredients until smooth by using a quick stirring motion or an electric mixer.

Apple Cheddar Muffins

1/2 c. solid shortening
1/2 c. sugar
2 large eggs
1 1/2 c. unbleached flour
1 tsp. baking powder
1 tsp. baking soda
1/2 tsp. salt
3/4 c. quick cooking oats
2/3 c. sharp cheddar cheese, grated
1/2 c. pecans, chopped
1 c. apples, finely chopped
3/4 c. milk
12–15 apple slices, unpeeled and thinly sliced
6 tbsp. butter, melted
1/2 c. cinnamon sugar

Preheat oven to 400°F.

Cream shortening and sugar together. Add the eggs, one at a time, beating well after each addition.

Combine the flour, baking powder, baking soda, and salt in a mixing bowl; mix lightly. Gradually stir the flour mixture into the shortening mixture. In this order, add the oats, cheese, pecans, and chopped apples, mixing well after each addition. Gradually add the milk, stirring until all the ingredients are just moistened.

Grease muffin pans and fill each cup two-thirds full of batter. Dip apple slices in melted butter and then into cinnamon sugar. Press 1 apple slice into the top of each muffin. Sprinkle lightly with cinnamon sugar and bake for 25 minutes, or until golden brown.

Apple Crunch Muffins

1 1/2 c. unbleached flour, sifted
1/2 c. sugar
2 tsp. baking powder
1/2 tsp. salt
1 1/2 tsp. ground cinnamon
1/4 c. vegetable shortening
1 large egg, slightly beaten
1/2 c. milk
1 c. tart apples, cored and shredded
Nut Crunch Topping (recipe follows)

Sift together flour, sugar, baking powder, salt, and cinnamon in a mixing bowl. Cut in shortening with pastry blender until fine crumbs form.

Combine egg and milk. Add to dry ingredients all at once, stirring just enough to moisten. Stir in apples.

Spoon batter into paper-lined, 2 1/2-inch muffin-pan cups, filling each cup two-thirds full. Sprinkle with Nut Crunch Topping. Bake in 375°F oven for 25 minutes, or until golden brown. Serve hot.

Yields 6–8 large muffins.

Nut Crunch Topping:
1/4 c. brown sugar, packed
1/4 c. chopped pecans
1/2 tsp. ground cinnamon

Mix all ingredients together to make topping.

Banana Bran Muffins

1 c. whole bran cereal
2/3 c. milk
1 large banana, mashed
1/4 c. cooking oil
1 egg, beaten
1 1/2 c. flour
1/2 c. brown sugar, packed
2 1/2 tsp. baking powder
1/2 tsp. salt
1/4 tsp. cloves

In large bowl, stir together cereal, milk, and banana. Let stand 2 minutes, or until cereal is soft. Add oil and egg; mix well. Stir dry ingredients into bran mixture until just moistened. Spoon into greased muffin cups. Bake at 375°F for 25–30 minutes.

Yields 6 large or 12 small muffins.

Banana Muffins

3 large bananas
3/4 c. sugar
1 egg, slightly beaten
1/3 c. butter, melted
1 tsp. baking soda
1 tsp. baking powder
1/2 tsp. salt
1 1/2 c. all-purpose flour

Mash bananas. Add sugar and slightly beaten egg; mix well. Add melted butter. Make a well in the middle and add dry ingredients. Pour into muffin pan. Bake at 375°F for 20 minutes.

*If you want to make the top a bit crunchy, sprinkle with brown sugar before baking.

Yields 12 muffins.

Blueberry Muffins

1/2 c. butter
1 1/4 c. sugar
2 eggs, slightly beaten
2 c. flour
2 tsp. baking powder
1/2 tsp. salt
1/2 c. milk
2 1/2 c. blueberries
sugar for topping

Cream butter and sugar. Add eggs and mix well. Sift dry ingredients and add to creamed mixture alternately with milk. Fold in blueberries. Pour into paper-lined muffin pan, dividing batter among 12 cups. Sprinkle with sugar. Bake at 375°F for 20–25 minutes. Cool in pan.

Note: Do not use blueberries in heavy syrup. If you want to use apples instead, use about 2 1/2 cups, chopped into small pieces and then sprinkled with cinnamon sugar.

Fat-Free Fruit Muffins

1 1/4 c. flour, white or whole wheat
1 c. oat bran or oatmeal
1 1/4 tsp. cinnamon
1 tbsp. baking powder
1/2 c. evaporated skim milk
1/2 c. defrosted apple juice concentrate
2 egg whites
1 ripe banana, mashed, or 1/2 cup applesauce
1 c. fruit (berries, diced peaches, pears,
   apples, raisins)

Mix dry ingredients. Stir together all wet ingredients except fruit. Blend together wet and dry ingredients, then add fruit. Spoon into greased muffin cups. Bake at 425°F for 15–17 minutes.
*Watch carefully as they will be dry if overcooked.

Nutty Banana Jam Muffins

1 1/4 c. ground walnuts, divided
1 1/2 c. sugar, divided
3/4 c. butter, softened
2 extra-ripe medium bananas, peeled
1 egg
2 c. flour
2 tsp. baking powder
1 1/2 tsp. ground cinnamon
1/2 tsp. ground nutmeg
1/4 tsp. salt
1 ripe small banana, peeled
3 tbsp. raspberry jam

Line eighteen 2 1/2-inch muffin cups with paper liners.

In shallow dish, combine 3/4 cup walnuts and 1/2 cup sugar; set aside.

In large bowl, beat remaining 1/2 cup nuts with remaining 1 cup sugar and butter until light and fluffy. Purée 2 medium bananas in blender (about 1 cup). Beat puréed bananas and egg into sugar-butter mixture. In medium bowl, combine flour, baking powder, cinnamon, nutmeg, and salt. Beat dry ingredients into banana mixture until well mixed.

Mash small banana in a separate bowl; stir in raspberry jam.

For each muffin, roll 1 heaping tablespoon of dough in walnut-sugar mixture to coat. Place in lined muffin cup. Make a dimple in the center of dough with back of spoon. Spoon 1 teaspoon jam mixture into center. Roll 1 more heaping tablespoon of dough in walnut-sugar mixture. Drop over jam mixture. Bake at 400°F for 15–20 minutes, or until wooden pick inserted in center comes out clean. Cool slightly in pan; place on wire rack to cool before serving. Serve warm.

Orange Muffins

1/2 c. butter, softened
1 c. sugar
2 eggs
3/4 c. sour cream
1/2 tsp. orange extract
2 c. all-purpose flour
1 tsp. baking soda
1/2 tsp. salt
1/2 c. pecans, chopped
3 tbsp. grated orange rind
3 tbsp. orange juice

Orange Icing:
2 c. confectioners' sugar
1 tbsp. butter, melted
1 tbsp. grated orange rind
1/4 c. orange juice

Cream the butter in a large mixing bowl. Add the sugar, beating until light and fluffy. Beat in the eggs. Stir in the sour cream and orange extract.

In a separate bowl, sift together the flour, soda, and salt. Blend the flour mixture into the butter mixture. Add the pecans, orange rind, and juice. Mix well.

Spray muffin tins with nonstick spray. Spoon the batter into the tins, filling each three-fourths full.

Bake at 375°F for 20 minutes. Cool and ice.

For the icing, place the sugar, butter, orange rind, and juice in the top of a double boiler over hot water for 10 minutes. Remove from heat. Beat the icing until it reaches the desired spreading consistency.

Dinner Rolls

Blend:

To thoroughly mix two or more ingredients.

Boil:

To raise the temperature of a liquid until it bubbles;
The boiling temperature of water is 212° F (or 100° C).

Kentucky Yeast Rolls

1 c. milk
5 tbsp. sugar
1 tsp. salt
4 tbsp. shortening
5 c. flour, divided
1 pkg. yeast, dissolved in 1/4 c. warm water
1 egg, slightly beaten

Warm milk, sugar, salt, and shortening in microwave for 1–2 minutes. Let cool. Shortening need not be melted. Set aside.

Put 2 cups of flour in a bowl. Add yeast, egg, and sugar mixture. Using electric mixer, beat well. Add flour 1/2 cup at a time until mixer can no longer turn, then stir with wooden spoon. Let dough rest 15 minutes on floured board.

Knead 15–20 times. Coat dough by rolling in butter-greased bowl. Cover and refrigerate until ready to use.

On floured board, knead dough 10 times. Divide into 24 balls. Place in greased pan. Let rise 1–2 hours or until dough doubles. Bake at 400°F for 10–15 minutes or until golden brown.

Remove from oven butter top of rolls. Serve hot.

Yields 2 dozen.

Refrigerator Rolls

1 pkg. yeast
1 c. warm milk
1/4 lb. butter or margarine
1/4 c. sugar
2 eggs, well beaten
4 c. sifted flour
1 tsp. salt

Dissolve yeast in warm milk. Cream butter and sugar until fluffy. Add yeast mixture, eggs, flour, and salt to butter mixture and mix well. Chill overnight. Remove from refrigerator 3 hours before serving time. Divide into 3 sections. Roll each section out on a floured surface into a 10-inch round that is 1/4 inch thick. Cut into 12 wedge-shaped pieces. Roll the wedges up from the round edge and ending with the point. Place on pan, point sides down, brush with oil, and let rise in warm place until doubled. Bake at 400°F for 8–10 minutes.

Bow-Knot Dinner Rolls

6 c. flour, divided
1/2 c. sugar
1/2 tsp. salt
2 pkgs. yeast
1 1/3 c. very warm water
10 tbsp. margarine, softened
3 eggs
poppy seeds

Mix 1 1/2 cups flour, sugar, salt, and undissolved yeast. Add water and margarine to dry ingredients. Beat 2 minutes at medium speed. Add 2 eggs and 1 cup flour. Beat 2 minutes at high speed. Stir in enough flour to make a dough.

Knead 8–10 minutes on a floured surface. Set in greased bowl; turn to grease top. Cover with plastic and refrigerate 2–24 hours. Punch down dough and divide into 48 pieces.

Roll each into an 8-inch rope and twist into a loose knot. Let rise 1 hour in warm place.

Beat remaining egg and brush over rolls. Sprinkle with poppy seeds. Bake at 400°F for 10–12 minutes.

Best-Ever Yeast Rolls

2 pkgs. dry yeast
2/3 c. sugar, divided
1 c. warm water
1 tsp. salt
1/2 c. butter, softened
1/2 c. shortening
1 c. boiling water
2 eggs, beaten
6–7 c. all-purpose flour, divided

Dissolve yeast and 1 teaspoon sugar in 1 cup warm water. Let stand about 5 minutes.

Combine remaining sugar, salt, butter, and shortening in a large bowl. Add boiling water, stirring until butter and shortening melt. Cool slightly. Add dissolved yeast, stirring well.

Add eggs and 3 cups flour, beating at medium speed with an electric mixer until smooth. Gradually stir in enough remaining flour to make a soft dough. Place in a well-greased bowl, turning to grease all over. Cover and let rise in a warm place, free from drafts, 1 to 1 1/2 hours, or until doubled in bulk.

Punch dough down and turn out on a well-floured surface, kneading several times. Shape into 2-inch balls and place in 3, greased, 9-inch round pans. Cover and let rise in a warm place, free from drafts, for 30–40 minutes or until doubled in bulk. Bake at 325°F for 20–25 minutes, or until golden. Yields 3 dozen.

Butter-Rich Dinner Rolls

1/4 c. warm water
2 tbsp. sugar
1 pkg. dry yeast
2 c. flour
6 tbsp. butter, melted, divided
1/4 tsp. salt
1 large egg
1/3 c. milk

Combine water, sugar, and yeast. Add flour and mix at slow speed until mixture is crumbly. Add 4 tablespoons melted butter, salt, and egg. Beat until well blended. Add milk and beat until thoroughly mixed. Cover bowl with plastic wrap and refrigerate until dough doubles in size (about 30 minutes).

Pour 1 tablespoon of melted butter into 8-inch round cake pan, turning to coat sides and bottom. Drop batter by spoonfuls into pan. Pour remaining butter over rolls and let rise 10 minutes. Bake at 350°F until golden brown.

Peanut Butter Rolls

1 cake compressed yeast
1/4 c. lukewarm water
1 c. milk, scalded
1/4 c. sugar
2 tsp. salt
1/4 c. shortening, melted
2 eggs, well beaten
1/4 tsp. nutmeg
1/2 c. peanut butter
3 1/2 c. flour

Preheat oven to 450°F.

Soften yeast in water. Add milk, sugar, salt, shortening, eggs, nutmeg, and peanut butter. Beat well. Add flour to make a dough that is just stiff enough to be kneaded. Turn out on a lightly floured board. Knead until smooth. Cover and let rise until doubled in bulk; work down. Form into rolls. Place on a well-oiled baking sheet. Cover and let rise until tripled in bulk. Bake for 15 minutes.

Sour Cream Rolls

1/4 c. warm water
1/4 c. butter
1 c. sour cream
3 c. flour, divided
1 pkg. active dry yeast
2 tbsp. sugar
1 tsp. salt
1 egg
oil
butter

In a small pan, heat warm water (105–110°F) and butter. Heat to melt butter but do not boil, then add sour cream. Heat until quite warm (110–120°F).

In a bowl mix together 1 cup flour, yeast, sugar, and salt. Mix thoroughly. Combine with liquid ingredients and mix vigorously by hand or with mixer. Add egg and continue beating. While beating add up to 2 cups flour or until you get a dough stiff enough to handle. Dough should be soft, but no longer sticky.

Oil top of dough, cover bowl with plastic wrap and let rise until nearly doubled in size (about 50–60 minutes).

Place dough on a floured board and pat out to about 1/2 inch thick. Cut and shape as you wish. Let rise 15–30 minutes. Bake at 375°F about 20 minutes. Butter the tops when they come out.

Note: These can be turned into "brown–and–serve" rolls and frozen. They are great when you just need one or two rolls. Bake until barely "ivory" in color, cool, and freeze. When you want to serve later, place in a pre-heated oven and bake until nicely browned.

Parker House Rolls

1 cake compressed yeast
3/4 c. milk, scalded and cooled
1 3/4 tsp. salt
1/4 c. shortening, melted
6 tbsp. sugar
3/4 c. water, lukewarm
5 1/4 c. flour

Preheat oven to 450°F.

Soften yeast in cooled milk. Add salt, shortening, sugar, and water. Add flour, a little at a time, beating thoroughly after each addition.

Turn out on a lightly floured board and knead until smooth.

Cover with a warm, damp cloth. Let rise until doubled in bulk.

Roll dough out until it is 1/3 inch thick. Cut in rounds 2 inches in diameter. Crease the middle of each with the dull edge of a knife.

Brush lightly with butter.

Fold over, pressing together with the palm of your hand.

Place close together in rows on a well-oiled baking sheet.

Cover and let rise until tripled in bulk.

Bake for 15–18 minutes.

Breads

Combine:
To stir together two or more ingredients.

Cream:
To beat a mixture with a spoon or electric mixer until it is smooth, light, fluffy, and nearly twice its original volume.

Bagels

Dough:

2 tbsp. plus 1 tsp. sugar, divided
3 c. plus 1 tbsp. flour, divided
2/3 c. lukewarm water
1 1/2 tbsp. dry yeast
2 eggs
1/4 c. vegetable oil
1 1/2 tsp. salt

Poaching Liquid:

16 c. water
2 tbsp. sugar

Glaze:

1 egg yolk
1 tbsp. water
poppy or sesame seeds

In a large bowl, combine 2 tablespoons sugar, 1 tablespoon flour, and 2/3 cup water. Sprinkle in yeast and let stand until frothy (2 minutes). Stir in eggs and oil. Mix 1 cup flour, 1 teaspoon sugar, and salt into yeast mixture. Beat with wooden spoon until smooth. Stir in enough of the remaining flour to make a soft dough.

Turn dough out on a lightly floured surface and knead until smooth and elastic (about 10 minutes). Place in a greased bowl. Roll dough around in the bowl to grease it all over. Cover with plastic wrap and let stand in a warm place to rise for 1 hour, or until doubled in size.

Punch down dough using fist and knead for 2 minutes. Divide into 12 equal portions. Shape each piece into a ball (keep remaining dough covered with plastic wrap while shaping). Poke finger through center of each ball.

Twirl around finger to form a ring. Place on floured oven tray and cover. Allow to rise for 15 minutes.

Bring 16 cups water to a boil in a large pan. Add 2 tablespoons sugar. Place half of the bagels in the water; cook 1 minute. Turn, and cook 1 minute longer. Using a slotted spoon, remove bagels to a greased baking tray lined with greased foil. Cook remaining half of bagels in poaching liquid.

Combine egg yolk and 1 tablespoon water. Brush over bagels. Sprinkle with poppy or sesame seeds. Bake at 400°F for 25 minutes, or until golden. Cool on a wire rack.

Makes 12.

English Muffin Bread

6 c. flour, divided
2 pkgs. yeast
1 tbsp. sugar
2 tsp. salt
1/4 tsp. baking soda
2 c. milk
1/2 c. water
cornmeal

Combine 3 cups flour, yeast, sugar, salt, and soda. Mix liquids together and heat until very warm (120–130°F). Add to dry mixture; beat well. Stir in rest of flour to make a stiff batter. Spoon into 2 loaf pans that have been greased and sprinkled with cornmeal. Cover and let rise in warm place for 45 minutes. Bake at 400°F for 25 minutes. Remove from pans immediately and cool.

Fat-Free Mexican Corn Bread

1 1/2 c. yellow cornmeal
1/2 c. white or whole wheat flour
1 tbsp. baking powder
2 egg whites
1 c. nonfat milk
1 (16-oz.) can creamed corn
1/4 c. chopped onion
2 tbsp. chopped red pepper or pimiento
1 small can chili peppers, chopped
1 tsp. chopped jalapeño chiles

Mix all dry ingredients. Mix all wet ingredients, onions, and peppers. Blend together. Pour into greased 8-inch square pan and bake at 425°F for 35–40 minutes. If using muffin pans, baking time should be cut in half.

Bacon Spoon Bread

3/4 c. cornmeal
1 1/2 c. cold water
2 c. shredded sharp cheddar cheese
1/4 c. butter, room temperature
2 cloves garlic, crushed
1/2 tsp. salt
1 c. milk
4 egg yolks
1/2 lb. fried bacon, crumbled
4 egg whites, beaten stiff

Preheat oven to 325°F. Stir cornmeal into cold water in a saucepan and place over medium heat. Bring to bubbling boil, stirring constantly. When thick, remove from heat. Stir in cheese, butter, garlic, and salt. When cheese is melted, add milk. Stir in egg yolks and bacon bits. Fold beaten egg whites into the batter. Pour into greased 2-quart casserole or soufflé dish. Level the batter. Bake for about 1 hour.

The bread should be nicely browned, high and puffy. Slip a knife blade into the center of the casserole. If the blade comes out clean and dry, the spoon bread is done. If not, return to the oven for an additional 10 minutes. Remove bread from the oven. Serve while hot.

Rich Egg Bread

2 pkgs. yeast
1/2 c. warm water
1 1/2 c. milk, scalded and cooled to lukewarm
1/4 c. sugar
1 tbsp. salt
3 eggs
1/4 c. shortening
7 to 7 1/2 c. flour, divided

Dissolve yeast in warm water in a large bowl that has been warmed. Stir in milk, sugar, salt, eggs, shortening, and 3 1/2 cups flour. Beat until smooth. Mix in enough flour to make dough easy to handle (3 1/2 to 4 cups). Turn out on a lightly floured surface and knead until smooth and elastic, about 10 minutes. Place in greased bowl and turn to coat dough all around. Cover and let rise for 1 to 1 1/2 hours, or until doubled in size.

Grease two loaf pans. Punch down the dough and divide in half. Roll each into a 9 x 18-inch rectangle. Roll up, beginning with the 9-inch side. Press ends to seal. Fold ends under and place seam side down into loaf pans. Cover and let rise until almost doubled in size.

Place oven rack in the lowest position. Bake loaves in preheated 425°F oven about 25–30 minutes or until loaves sound hollow when tapped.

Makes 2 loaves.

Old-Fashioned White Bread

1 pkg. yeast
1/2 c. warm water
2 tbsp. sugar
2 tsp. salt
2 tbsp. shortening
1 c. very hot water
1 c. milk
5 c. all-purpose flour

Dissolve yeast in 1/2 cup warm water. Place sugar, salt, and shortening in a bowl. Add 1 cup very hot water and stir to dissolve. Add milk and yeast to bowl. Add enough flour to make a stiff dough. Knead until smooth but not sticky. Place in greased bowl and let rise until doubled in size. Shape into two loaves and place in bread pans. Let rise until doubled in bulk.

Bake at 400°F for 35–40 minutes, or until golden and hollow sounding when tapped lightly on top.

French Onion Bread

1 3/4 c. boiling water
3 tbsp. sugar
3 tbsp. butter
2 tsp. salt
1 pkg. dry onion soup mix
1/2 c. warm water
2 tbsp. yeast
2 tsp. sugar
6 c. flour
melted butter

Pour boiling water into a large bowl. Add 3 tablespoons sugar, butter, salt, and onion soup mix. Stir and let cool until mixture is lukewarm. In small bowl mix in 1/2 cup warm water, yeast, and 2 teaspoons sugar. Add to ingredients in large bowl. Stir.

Work in enough flour until dough pulls away from the sides of the bowl. Knead about 10 minutes. Place in greased bowl, cover with a towel, and put in oven with light on to rise. When doubled in size, punch down and form into loaves. Cover again and let rise in oven until doubled in size. Bake at 375°F until golden brown. Brush tops with melted butter.

Homemade Pizza Dough

1 pkg. dry yeast
1/4 c. warm water
2 tsp. sugar
1 1/2 c. water
6 1/2 c. flour
1 tbsp. oil

Mix yeast, 1/4 cup warm water, and sugar in a bowl; let sit 5 minutes.

Add sugar and 1 1/2 cups water; stir together. Gradually add flour 1 cup at a time, mixing until dough is firm.

Knead dough in bowl approximately 10 times. Oil bowl and knead dough in oil a couple of times.

Let rise until doubled. Transfer dough to 1 large or 2 round pizza pans.

Top with your favorite toppings.

Bake in a 400°F oven for approximately 20–30 minutes, or until crispy.

Biscuits & Scones

Cut In:

To mix a solid fat, such as butter, with dry ingredients using a pastry cutter, food processor, or two knives.

Dough:

A thick mixture of flour and liquid that is combined with other ingredients to make recipes such as cookies or bread.

Fluffy Biscuits

2 c. plain flour
1/2 tsp. salt
1 tsp. sugar
1/4 tsp. baking soda
1 tbsp. baking powder
5 tbsp. shortening
1 c. buttermilk

Preheat oven to 450°F. Sift dry ingredients. Cut in shortening with pastry cutter. Make a well in the middle and pour in buttermilk. Using a fork, lightly mix until flour is moistened thoroughly. On floured surface, knead three times. Pat dough out until 1/2 inch thick. Cut into rounds with an inverted drinking glass or a biscuit cutter. Set biscuits in a greased pan so that their edges touch. Bake 12–15 minutes at 450°F.

Buttermilk Scones

2 1/4 c. flour
2 tbsp. sugar
2 1/2 tsp. baking powder
1/2 tsp. baking soda
1/2 tsp. salt
1/2 c. cold butter, cubed
1 c. buttermilk
1 egg, slightly beaten

Preheat oven to 425°F.

Mix flour, sugar, baking powder, baking soda, and salt in the bowl of a food processor. Add butter and process until the mixture resembles coarsely ground meal. Transfer to a bowl. (Use a pastry cutter if you don't have a food processor.)

Add buttermilk, stirring quickly with a fork until the dough is soft and slightly sticky. With floured hands, press the dough into a ball. Knead delicately a dozen times. Flatten the dough into a 1-inch thick circle. Cut into 3-inch disks. Repeat with remaining dough. Brush the scones with egg. Bake 12–15 minutes.

Orange Date Scones

1 3/4 c. flour
3/4 tsp. baking powder
1/4 tsp. baking soda
1/2 tsp. salt
1/2 c. sugar
1 tsp. orange peel
1/2 c. butter
2/3 c. chopped dates
1 egg
2 tbsp. milk
1/2 tsp. vanilla extract

Combine all dry ingredients. Cut in butter, add dates. Combine all liquids, and beat slightly to break up the egg; add to dry ingredients.

Gently shape dough into a ball. Place on floured board and pat into a large circle about 1/2 inch thick.

Cut into wedges, place on baking sheet, and bake at 350°F for 15–20 minutes.

Orange Poppy Seed Scones

2 1/4 c. flour
3/4 tsp. baking soda
1/2 tsp. salt
1 tsp. cream of tartar
1/2 c. sugar
1/4 c. poppy seed
1 tsp. orange peel
1/2 c. butter
1 large egg
1/4 c. orange juice

Preheat oven to 375°F.

Mix all dry ingredients together. Using pastry cutter, cut butter into flour mixture until it resembles coarse cornmeal.

Beat the egg slightly into the orange juice; add liquid mixture to dry mixture and gently shape dough into a ball. Cut the ball in half. Pat each half out on a floured surface into a circle about 1/2 inch thick and 8 inches across. Cut into wedges and place on a baking sheet. Bake 15–20 minutes, or until golden brown.

Cheese Scones

2 c. flour
2 tsp. baking powder
1/2 tsp. salt
1/8 tsp. cayenne pepper
1 1/2 c. grated cheddar cheese
3 tbsp. Parmesan cheese
1/3 c. butter
2 eggs
1/3 c. milk

Preheat oven to 400°F.

Combine all dry ingredients. Stir in cheeses and toss well.

Cut in butter. Combine eggs and milk; add to flour mixture and gently knead to form a stiff dough.

Cut dough ball into halves and pat each half into a circle about 1/2 inch thick and 8 inches across. Cut into wedges and place on a baking sheet. Bake 15–17 minutes, or until lightly browned.

Purely Scones

2 c. self-rising flour
1/2 tsp. baking soda
3/4 c. buttermilk
milk or egg for glaze, if desired

Preheat oven to 350°F.

Sift self-rising flour at least once into the mixing bowl. Stir soda into buttermilk until it begins to foam. Pour into well in center of flour and stir with fork, incorporating just enough flour to make a very soft dough. Gather into ball and place on lightly floured board. Pat or roll into a circle, kneading very lightly.

Using a spatula, cut into 8 or 10 wedges. Transfer to greased baking sheet. To give scones a shine, brush with milk. For a golden gleam, brush with an egg yolk beaten with a tablespoon of water. Bake for 10–12 minutes in the upper third of oven. Wrap in linen napkin, tuck into basket, and serve soon.

Makes 8–10 scones.

Scottish Oat Scones

1 1/2 c. uncooked old-fashioned oats
1 1/2 c. flour
1 tbsp. baking powder
1 tsp. cream of tartar
2 tbsp. sugar
1/2 c. raisins or currants
1 stick margarine, melted
1/3 c. milk
1 egg, beaten

Mix together all dry ingredients. Mix together wet ingredients then add to the dry ingredients. Mix with a fork until just moistened (do not over mix). Form into a ball, and then flatten on a greased cookie sheet into a circle about 8 inches across. Cut into 8 or 12 wedges. Bake 12–15 minutes at 425°F. Cool on a rack.

Treacle Scones

2 c. all-purpose flour
1/4 c. dark brown sugar, firmly packed
1 1/2 tsp. baking powder
1/2 tsp. baking soda
1/4 tsp. ground cinnamon
1/4 tsp. ground nutmeg
1/4 tsp. salt
1/2 c. dried currants
1/4 c. (1/2 stick) unsalted butter
2 tbsp. dark molasses
3/4 c. buttermilk
melted butter
sugar

Preheat oven to 425°F. Sift flour, dark brown sugar, baking powder, baking soda, cinnamon, nutmeg, and salt into a large bowl. Add dried currants. Melt unsalted butter with dark molasses in a heavy saucepan over low heat.

Combine molasses mixture with buttermilk and pour into dry ingredients. Mix dough until just blended.

Gently knead dough on generously floured surface until smooth, about 20 turns. Divide dough in half. Pat out each dough piece into 5-inch diameter rounds. Cut each dough round into 4 wedges. Transfer dough wedges to ungreased cookie sheet, spacing 2 inches apart. Brush with melted butter. Sprinkle with sugar. Bake until scones are just firm to the touch, about 20 minutes. Serve scones hot.

Makes 8 scones.

Wheat and Herb Scones

1 1/2 c. all-purpose flour
1 1/2 c. whole wheat flour
1 tbsp. baking powder
1 tsp. dry basil leaves
1/2 tsp. dry oregano leaves
1/2 tsp. dry thyme leaves
1/2 c. butter or margarine
2 large eggs
1/2 c. milk

In a large bowl, mix dry ingredients. Add butter, and cut into flour mixture with a pastry cutter. Beat eggs and milk to blend; set aside 2 tablespoons of egg-milk mixture. Add remainder to flour mixture, and stir until just evenly moistened.

Scrape dough out on a floured board or surface, and knead about 6 turns or until dough holds together. Divide dough in half. Pat each half into a 3/4-inch thick round, 5–6 inches in diameter. Set rounds well apart on a greased 12 x 15–inch baking sheet. With a knife, cut each round not quite through, to form 6 equal wedges. Brush rounds with reserved egg-milk mixture. Bake in a 400°F oven until golden brown, about 18 minutes. Serve hot.

Maple Syrup Biscuits

4 tbsp. butter, melted
1/2 c. maple syrup
1 c. flour
2 tsp. baking powder
1/4 tsp. salt
3 tbsp. butter, cold
1/3 c. milk

Pour the melted butter and syrup in a 9-inch cake pan, swirling to mix well.

Sift together the flour, baking powder, and salt. Cut in the cold butter, until the mixture resembles soft bread crumbs. Stir in the milk.

Turn the dough out and knead it gently until it just holds together.

Roll the dough out so that it is 1/2 inch thick, then cut it into rounds.

Arrange the rounds in the prepared cake pan on top of the butter-syrup mixture.

Bake at 375°F for 12–15 minutes, or until the biscuits are lightly browned and the syrup is bubbling up around the biscuits.

Serve immediately.

Sweet Potato Biscuits

1 (10-oz.) sweet potato, unpeeled
6 tbsp butter, melted
1/2 c. milk
2 tbsp. sugar
1 large egg, beaten
1 1/4 c. cake flour
1 1/4 c. all-purpose flour
1 tbsp. plus 1 tsp. baking powder
1/2 tsp. salt

Preheat the oven to 425°F.

Boil the entire sweet potato in unsalted water for 20–30 minutes, or until tender.

Allow the potato to cool. When cool, pare and mash it until smooth so that you have approximately 1 cup of mashed sweet potato.

Allow the cooking water to cool to warm.

Stir the mashed potato with the melted butter until smooth. Stir in the milk, sugar, and egg.

In a separate bowl, sift together the cake and all-purpose flours, baking powder, and salt. Then stir the flour mixture into the liquids to combine. Knead briefly in the bowl to form a soft dough. Turn the dough out on a lightly floured surface. Roll it out and cut it into rounds.

Transfer the biscuits to an ungreased baking sheet. Bake for 15–20 minutes, or until golden brown.

Whole Wheat Biscuits

1 c. whole wheat flour
1 c. all-purpose flour
1 tbsp. baking powder
3/4 tsp. salt
1/3 c. solid shortening
3/4 c. milk

Preheat oven to 450°F.

Combine the dry ingredients and mix well. Cut in the shortening. Add the milk to make a soft dough. Place the dough on a lightly floured board, and pat or roll out until it is 1/2-inch thick. Cut into biscuit rounds. Bake for 15 minutes.

Irish Breakfast Scones

1 1/2 c. whole wheat pastry flour
1/3 c. flour
3/4 c. wheat bran
1 tsp. baking powder
2 tbsp. butter or margarine
2 tbsp. corn syrup
1 c. soy milk

Preheat oven to 400°F.

Mix dry ingredients. Add the butter and mix well. Add the syrup and just enough milk to make a loose dough. Turn out on a lightly floured board and knead until smooth. Roll out into a square that is 3/4 inch thick. Cut dough in half, then into quarters, and then to eighths. Bake on a lightly floured baking sheet for approximately 20 minutes. Cool on a wire rack. Split and serve.

Blueberry Scones

3/4 c. blueberries, dried
1 3/4 c. flour, sifted
2 1/4 tsp. baking powder
1 tbsp. sugar
1/2 tsp. salt
1/4 c. butter
2 eggs
1/3 c. cream

Preheat oven to 450°F.

Place blueberries in a bowl with enough hot water to cover. Soak for about 5 minutes; drain.

In a bowl, mix the flour, baking powder, sugar, and salt. Cut in the butter, using a pastry blender or two knives. Stir in the blueberries.

In a separate bowl, beat the eggs. Reserve 2 tablespoons of the eggs. Add the remaining eggs to the dry ingredients. Pour in the cream. Combine with a few swift strokes.

Place on a lightly floured board and pat or roll out until it is 3/4 inch thick. Using a knife, cut the dough into diamond shapes or 2-inch rounds. Brush with the reserved egg and sprinkle with additional sugar. Bake for 15 minutes.

Date Scones

1 1/2 c. all-purpose flour
1/2 c. whole-wheat flour
1/4 c. bran
2 tsp. baking powder
1/2 tsp. baking soda
1 tsp. salt
2 tsp. cinnamon
1/4 c. brown sugar
1/2 c. unsalted butter, chilled
1 egg
2/3 c. buttermilk
2/3 c. chopped dates

Preheat oven to 350°F.

Combine the flours, bran, baking powder, soda, salt, cinnamon, and brown sugar. Cut in the butter. Add the egg, buttermilk, and dates; do not over mix. (If the dough seems too sticky, add a little more flour.)

On a lightly floured surface, shape the dough into a 1-inch thick rectangle. Cut the dough into 12 triangles. Bake on an ungreased baking sheet for 25 minutes. Cool on a rack.

Bars & Brownies

Dredge:
To coat, usually with flour.

Drizzle:
To pour a liquid, such as butter, over food in a thin stream.

Dust:
To lightly sprinkle an ingredient, such as confectioners' sugar, over a food.

Chocolate Fudge Michelle

Bake this cake at least 2 days ahead. The flavor and texture improve on standing.

6 oz. unsweetened chocolate
6 tbsp. strong-brewed coffee
1 tbsp. vanilla extract
3/4 lb. (3 sticks) butter, softened
1 lb. dark brown sugar
1 c. granulated sugar
6 large eggs, separated
1 c. sifted all-purpose flour
confectioners' sugar for decorating
1 c. heavy cream, whipped (optional)

Adjust the rack to center of the oven and preheat to 350°F. Butter a 10-inch springform pan. In a double boiler, over simmering water, melt the chocolate with the coffee. Remove from heat. When slightly cool, stir in vanilla extract.

In a large bowl, cream the butter with the sugars until light and fluffy. Separate the eggs, placing the whites in a large bowl. Add the egg yolks, one at a time, to the butter-sugar mixture, beating well after each addition. Add the chocolate mixture to the batter and mix well. Stir in the flour, mixing only until incorporated.

Using clean, dry beaters, beat the egg whites until stiff and glossy but not dry. Gently fold the beaten egg whites into the chocolate mixture, being careful not to deflate them. Fold only until no white streaks remain. Gently turn the batter into the prepared pan. Smooth the top and bake for 1 hour, or until the top springs back when lightly touched. Remove from oven and cover top of cake with foil to keep it from hardening.

Place the pan on a rack to cool. When completely cool, store at room temperature, covered, in the baking pan until ready to serve.

At serving time, remove the sides of the springform pan and place the cake on a 12-inch cake platter. Dust the top lightly with confectioners' sugar. Top each portion with a dollop of whipped cream.

Black Bottom Cupcakes

Creamy Filling:
8 oz. cream cheese, softened
1 egg
1/3 c. sugar
1/8 tsp. salt
1 c. semi-sweet chocolate chips

Using a wooden spoon, blend cream cheese, egg, sugar, and salt. Carefully fold in chocolate chips. Set aside.

Cupcake:
1 1/2 c. flour, sifted
1 c. sugar
1/4 c. cocoa
1 tsp. baking soda
1/2 tsp. salt
1 c. water
1/3 c. vegetable oil
1 tbsp. white vinegar
1 tsp. vanilla extract

Combine dry ingredients in large bowl and mix well. Add remaining ingredients and blend thoroughly. Line a muffin pan with papers and fill each three-fourths full. Drop 1 heaping tablespoon of filling into center of each. Bake 25–30 minutes in a 375°F oven.

Grandma's Applesauce Bars

1/2 c. butter, softened
2 c. sugar
2 eggs
2 1/2 c. sifted all-purpose flour
1 1/2 tsp. baking soda
1 tsp. salt
1 tsp. cinnamon
1/2 tsp. nutmeg
1/4 tsp. allspice
1 1/2 c. applesauce
1/2 c. raisins
1/2 c. pecans

Cream butter and sugar until light. Add eggs, beating well after each addition. Sift dry ingredients together and add to creamed mixture alternately with applesauce. Stir in raisins and pecans. Turn batter into greased and lightly floured 13 x 9 x 2-inch pan. Bake at 350°F about 45 minutes, or until done. Cool in pan.

Raspberry Brownies

1/4 c. butter
4 oz. unsweetened chocolate
8 oz. cream cheese, softened
4 eggs
2 c. sugar
1 c. flour
1 jar raspberry preserves

Melt butter and chocolate together. Let cool.

Meanwhile, beat cream cheese with 1 egg, then set aside. Beat remaining 3 eggs, and add to the cooled chocolate mixture. Add sugar and flour.

Pour half this batter into an ungreased 9 x 13-inch pan. Top with the cream cheese mixture, then with the preserves. Cover with the rest of the batter. Bake at 350°F for 30–40 minutes.

Almond Bars

Crust:
1 c. butter
2 c. flour
1/2 c. confectioners' sugar

Mix well and pat into an even layer in a 9 x 13-inch pan. Bake crust at 350°F for 20–25 minutes.

Filling:
8 oz. cream cheese, softened
2 eggs
1/2 c. sugar
1 tsp. almond extract

Beat together all ingredients and pour over crust while it is still hot. Bake 15–20 minutes at 350°F and allow to cool.

Frosting:
1 1/2 c. confectioners' sugar
1/4 c. butter
1 1/2 tbsp. milk
1 tsp. almond extract

Whisk ingredients together and spread evenly over baked, cooled cookies. Cut into bars.

Yields 24–36 bars.

Brownie Boomers

4 oz. unsweetened chocolate
1 stick unsalted butter, room temperature
1 1/4 c. plus 1 tbsp. sugar
1/2 tsp. vanilla extract
3 large eggs, room temperature
3/4 c. all-purpose flour
Cream Cheese Filling (recipe follows)

Preheat oven to 300°F. Lightly grease an 8-inch square pan with butter or vegetable oil.

Melt the chocolate and butter in the top of a double boiler placed over simmering water. Cool mixture for 5 minutes.

Place sugar in a medium-sized mixing bowl and pour in the chocolate mixture. Using an electric mixer on medium speed, mix until blended, scraping the sides of the bowl with a rubber spatula.

Add vanilla extract. With mixer on medium-low speed, add eggs, one at a time, blending after each addition until the yolk is broken and dispersed. Scrape the bowl after the last egg and blend until smooth.

Add flour and mix on low speed for 20 seconds. Finish the mixing by hand, being certain to mix in any flour at the bottom of the bowl. Set aside.

Cream Cheese Filling:
8 oz. cream cheese, chilled
1 1/2 tsp. all-purpose flour
5 tbsp. sugar
1 large egg, room temperature
1/4 tsp. vanilla extract

Place all filling ingredients in a food processor and process until blended, about 45 seconds. Set aside.

Spread about 2/3 of the brownie batter in the prepared pan. Spread the Cream Cheese Filling over the brownie batter. Using a spoon, ladle the remaining brownie batter over the filling in nine equal mounds arranged in rows of threes so that there is some space between them.

Run a chopstick or the handle of a wooden spoon back and forth the length of the pan, making parallel lines about 1 1/2 inches apart. Then do the same thing in the other direction as if making a grid. This will marbleize the two mixtures. Shake the pan gently back and forth to level the batter.

Bake the bars on the center oven rack until a tester in the center comes out clean or with some moist crumbs, about 50 minutes. Allow the brownies to cool for 1 hour before cutting.

Cheerio Krisp Bars

1 c. Karo Syrup
1 c. sugar
1 c. crunchy peanut butter
1 c. chocolate chips
6 c. Cheerios or Rice Krispies cereal

Mix syrup and sugar in saucepan and bring to just boiling. Make sure sugar is completely dissolved. Remove from heat and immediately add peanut butter and chocolate chips. Stir in cereal and pour into pan, spreading to even out bars. Allow to cool before cutting into bars.

Cream Cheese Brownies

1 (4-oz.) pkg. German sweet chocolate
5 tbsp. butter, divided
1 (3-oz.) pkg. cream cheese, softened
1/4 c. sugar
3 eggs
1 tbsp. flour
1/2 tsp. vanilla extract
3/4 c. sugar
1/2 tsp. baking powder
1/4 tsp. salt
1/2 c. flour
1/2 c. coarsely chopped nuts
1 tsp. vanilla extract

Melt chocolate with 3 tablespoons of butter over very low heat, stirring constantly until smooth. Cool.

In a separate bowl, cream remaining 2 tablespoons butter with cream cheese until smooth. Gradually add 1/4 cup sugar, creaming until light and fluffy. Blend in 1 egg, 1 tablespoon flour, and 1/2 teaspoon vanilla extract.

In a separate bowl, beat remaining 2 eggs until light and fluffy. Gradually beat in 3/4 cup sugar, and continue beating until thickened. Stir in baking powder, salt, and 1/2 cup flour. Blend in chocolate. Stir in nuts and 1 teaspoon vanilla extract.

Spread half the chocolate batter in a greased 8- or 9-inch square pan. Spread cheese mixture over the top. Drop remaining chocolate batter by tablespoonfuls on top. Swirl through batters with a spatula to marbelize. Bake at 350°F for 35–40 minutes. Cool in pan. Cut into squares or bars.

Black Forest Chocolate Cups

1 (12-oz.) pkg. semi-sweet chocolate chips
2 tbsp. black cherry preserves
1/2 c. milk chocolate chips
1/4 c. confectioners' sugar
1 tsp. water
red food coloring

Stir semi-sweet chocolate chips in a medium-size, heavy saucepan over very low heat until melted and smooth. Spoon about 1/2 teaspoon of the melted chocolate into each of twenty-four 1-inch paper or foil bonbon cups. Drop about 1/4 teaspoon preserves into each cup. Spoon enough of the remaining melted chocolate into each cup to fill to the top. Set the cups aside.

Stir milk chocolate chips in a small, heavy saucepan over very low heat until melted and smooth. Remove from heat and set aside.

Stir the confectioners' sugar and 1/2 to 1 teaspoon of water in a small bowl until blended and smooth. Add a drop of food coloring, stirring to a light pink color. Spoon the melted milk chocolate and the icing into separate heavy-duty sandwich bags. Seal or twist the bags shut; cut a tiny hole in one corner of each. Pipe icing in lines across the tops of the chocolate cups. Pipe chocolate in lines crosswise to the icing.

Refrigerate at least 30 minutes until set. Store in an airtight container in the refrigerator for up to 1 week.

Makes 2 dozen cups.

No-Bake Peanut Butter Bars

3/4 c. butter, softened
1 lb. confectioners' sugar
2 c. peanut butter
1 1/2 c. crushed graham crackers
6 oz. chocolate chips
1 tbsp. vegetable oil

In a bowl, mix the butter, sugar, peanut butter, and crushed crackers, kneading until smooth. Press into 9 x 13-inch pan.

Melt the chocolate chips in a saucepan with the oil. Spread the melted chocolate over the mixture in the pan. Chill for 1 hour and cut into bars.

Banana Sour Cream Bars

1/2 c. butter, softened
1 1/2 c. sugar
2 eggs
3/4 c. sour cream
2 large ripe bananas, mashed
1 tsp. vanilla extract
1/2 tsp. salt
1 tsp. baking soda
2 c. flour

Preheat oven to 375°F.

Cream together the butter and sugar. Add the eggs, one at a time, beating well after each addition. Add the sour cream and mix. Add the mashed bananas, vanilla extract, salt, baking soda, and flour.

Bake in 15 x 10 x 2-inch jelly roll pan for 20–30 minutes.

Lemon Bars

3/4 c. flour
1/3 c. butter, softened
2 eggs
2 c. brown sugar
1/2 c. walnuts
1/8 tsp. baking powder
1/2 tsp. vanilla extract
2/3 c. confectioners' sugar
1 tsp. grated lemon rind
1 1/2 tbsp. lemon juice

Preheat oven to 350°F.

Mix the flour and butter until fine crumbs form.

Pat the mixture into an 11 x 7-inch pan.

Bake for 10 minutes.

In a bowl, beat the eggs.

Mix in the brown sugar, nuts, baking powder, and vanilla extract. Spread over the hot crumb mixture.

Bake for 20 minutes.

In a separate bowl, mix together the confectioners' sugar, lemon rind, and juice.

Spread over the hot cake.

Cool well and cut into squares.

Cakes

Fold:
To gently combine two mixtures using a spatula
in a light, circular motion.

Glaze:
To give food a shiny coating by applying a thin layer
of syrup, beaten egg, or milk.

Carrot Cake

1 1/3 c. flour
1/2 tsp. salt
1 1/3 tsp. baking powder
1 1/3 tsp. baking soda
1 1/3 tsp. cinnamon
1/2 tsp. cloves
1/2 tsp. ginger
1 c. sugar
1 c. cooking oil
3 eggs
2 c. grated carrots
1 c. chopped walnuts
Icing (recipe follows)

Preheat oven to 300°F.

Mix together flour, salt, baking powder, baking soda, cinnamon, cloves, and ginger; set aside. In separate bowl, mix sugar, cooking oil, and eggs. Add the dry ingredients to the wet mixture and stir well. Fold in carrots and walnuts.

Pour into a 9 x 13-inch nonstick pan. Bake for 50–60 minutes, or until done. Let cool and spread icing over cake before serving.

Icing:
1 (8-oz.) pkg. cream cheese, softened
1/2 c. butter, softened
1 1/2 c. confectioners' sugar

Mix together cream cheese and butter. Add sugar slowly and mix well. Spread on cooled cake.

Black Forest Cake

4 1/2 c. milk, divided
3 oz. unsweetened chocolate
1/3 c. cornstarch
1/2 c. sugar
1/4 tsp. salt
2 tsp. vanilla extract
2 c. cookie crumbs (made from vanilla wafers, shortbread, or chocolate chip cookies)
1 (20-oz.) can cherry pie filling, divided

Put 4 cups of milk into a large, heavy saucepan. Add unsweetened chocolate and heat over moderate heat, watching carefully, until bubbles form on milk around edges of pan. Remove from heat and set aside.

Mix cornstarch, sugar, salt, and remaining 1/2 cup milk in a small bowl. Use a whisk to stir mixture until all dry ingredients are moistened and no lumps remain.

Using a whisk, stir chocolate mixture in saucepan while gradually adding cornstarch mixture. Return saucepan to heat and cook over moderately high heat, stirring constantly, until mixture begins to boil. Boil 1 minute, stirring constantly. Remove from heat and stir in vanilla extract. Spoon one-third of pudding into a 2-quart soufflé dish or glass bowl. Top with one-third of cookie crumbs.

Set aside 1/2 cup cherry pie filling. Gently spoon half of remaining pie filling over the crumbs in the bowl. Repeat layering with another third of chocolate pudding, crumbs, the remaining pie filling, and the remaining chocolate pudding. Spoon remaining cookie crumbs around chocolate pudding to form a border. Fill center with reserved 1/2 cup of pie filling. Cover and refrigerate until pudding is well chilled, 5–6 hours.

Death By Chocolate

2 c. flour
1 tbsp. double-acting baking powder
1/2 tsp. baking soda
2 c. sugar
2 large eggs
1 stick unsalted butter, room temperature,
  quartered
1 c. sour cream
1/2 c. water
2 tsp. vanilla extract
1/2 c. plus 2 tbsp. cocoa
1 (12-oz) pkg. semi-sweet chocolate chips
confectioners' sugar

Sift flour, baking powder, and baking soda twice.
Place in a small bowl. Beat the sugar and eggs in
a large mixing bowl until sugar is dissolved. Add
butter and mix into egg mixture thoroughly. Add
sour cream, water, and vanilla extract; beat. Add
flour mixture and cocoa; beat slowly just until
flour is absorbed. Do not over beat.

Fold in chocolate chips and pour into buttered
Bundt pan. Bake at 350°F for 1 hour.

When cool, sift confectioners' sugar over the top.

German Chocolate Cake

4 oz. German sweet chocolate
1/2 c. boiling water
1 c. butter
2 c. sugar
4 egg yolks
4 egg whites, beaten stiff

1 tsp. vanilla extract
2 1/2 c. flour
1 tsp. baking soda
1/2 tsp. salt
1 c. buttermilk
Coconut Pecan Frosting (recipe follows)

Melt chocolate in boiling water. Cream butter and
sugar until fluffy. Add egg yolks, vanilla extract,
and chocolate. Add dry ingredients alternately with
buttermilk. Fold in egg whites.

Pour into three 9-inch pans, each lined with wax
paper. Bake at 350°F for 30–35 minutes. Frost tops
with Coconut Pecan Frosting, leaving sides
unfrosted.

Coconut Pecan Frosting:
1 c. evaporated milk
1 c. sugar
3 egg yolks
1/2 c. butter
1 tsp. vanilla extract
1 1/3 c. coconut
1 c. chopped pecans

Combine all except coconut and pecans in a
saucepan. Cook over medium heat, stirring
constantly, about 12 minutes. When mixture
thickens, remove from heat. Stir in coconut and
pecans. Cool until spreadable.

German Surprise Chocolate Cake

2/3 c. shortening
1 1/2 c. sugar
3 eggs
1 c. beer
1/2 c. cocoa
2 1/4 c. flour
1 1/2 tsp. salt
1 tsp. baking soda
1 tsp. baking powder
2/3 c. sauerkraut
German Surprise Frosting (recipe follows)

Cream shortening and sugar together. Add eggs, one at a time. Add beer and cocoa. Sift together flour, salt, soda, and baking powder; add to creamed mixture slowly, until all is mixed. Fold in sauerkraut.

Pour into a lightly greased 9 x 15-inch baking pan. Bake for 30–45 minutes at 375°F. Allow to cool before frosting with German Surprise Frosting.

German Surprise Frosting
1 (8-oz.) pkg. cream cheese, softened
2 tbsp. cream
1 tsp. vanilla extract
1/2 c. confectioners' sugar

Mix together cream cheese, cream, and vanilla extract. Add sugar slowly and mix well. Spread over top of cooled cake.

Buttermilk Chocolate Cake

2 c. flour
2 c. sugar
1/2 tsp. salt
1/2 c. margarine
1 c. water
1/2 c. vegetable shortening
3 tbsp. cocoa
2 eggs, beaten
1 tsp. baking soda
1/2 c. buttermilk
1 tsp. vanilla extract
2 tbsp. peanut butter
Icing (recipe follows)

Combine flour, sugar, and salt in large mixing bowl. Set aside. In saucepan, mix margarine, water, shortening, and cocoa and bring to a boil. Mix with flour mixture. In another bowl mix eggs, baking soda, buttermilk, and vanilla extract. Add this to hot mixture, and mix well.

Bake in greased and floured 9 x 13-inch pan at 350°F for 15–20 minutes. While cake is *hot* spread with a very thin layer of peanut butter. Then spread with icing.

Icing:
1/2 c. margarine
3 tbsp. cocoa
1 (6-oz.) box confectioners' sugar
1 tsp. vanilla extract
1/2 c. chopped nuts
6 tbsp. milk

Melt margarine and cocoa in saucepan, but *do not boil*. Mix well. Remove from heat and add confectioners' sugar, vanilla extract, nuts, and milk (add just enough milk to make the icing thin enough to spread). Mix well. *Ice cake while it is still hot.*

Mallo-Nut Fudge Cake

3 oz. baking chocolate, cut fine
3/4 c. boiling water
1 3/4 c. sifted cake flour
1 1/2 c. sugar
3/4 tsp. salt
1/2 tsp. baking powder
3/4 tsp. soda
1/2 c. shortening
1/3 c. thick sour milk
1 tsp. vanilla extract
2 eggs, unbeaten
18 large marshmallows, cut in half,
  or 1 1/2 c. miniature marshmallows
1/2 c. nuts
Minute Fudge Frosting (recipe follows)

Put chocolate in mixing bowl. Pour boiling water over chocolate and stir until melted. Cool. Sift flour, sugar, salt, baking powder, and soda into chocolate mixture. Drop in shortening. Beat 2 minutes at medium speed. Add sour milk, vanilla extract, and eggs; beat 2 minutes more. Bake at 350°F for 30–40 minutes in a 9 x 13-inch pan.

While still warm, put marshmallows and nuts on top of cake. Cool. Frost with Minute Fudge Frosting.

Minute Fudge Frosting:

1 oz. semi-sweet chocolate, cut fine
1 c. sugar
1/3 c. milk
1/4 c. shortening
1/4 tsp. salt
1 tsp. vanilla extract

Combine all ingredients except vanilla extract in a saucepan. Bring to a full rolling boil, stirring constantly. Let mixture boil for 1 minute. Remove from heat and stir until just warm. Add vanilla extract, then beat with mixer on high until thick enough to spread.

Best Fudge Cake

3/4 c. butter or margarine
2 1/4 c. light brown sugar, lightly packed
3 eggs
1 1/2 tsp. vanilla extract
3 oz. baking chocolate, melted squares
2 tsp. baking soda
1/2 tsp. salt
2 1/4 c. sifted cake flour
1 c. dairy sour cream
1 c. boiling water

In a large bowl, cream butter until smooth. Add brown sugar and eggs. Beat with mixer until light and fluffy, about 5 minutes. With mixer on low speed, beat in vanilla extract and chocolate, then baking soda and salt.

Add flour alternately with sour cream, beating on low speed until smooth. Pour in boiling water; stir with spoon until blended. Pour into greased and floured pan. Bake 35 minutes or until done.

Makes one 9 x 13-inch sheet cake or one 2-layer, 9-inch round cake.

Lemon Cheese Bundt Cake

2 sticks margarine, softened
1 stick butter, softened
1 (8-oz.) pkg. cream cheese, softened
6 eggs, divided
3 c. cake flour, sifted, divided
3 c. granulated sugar, divided
1/4 tsp. vanilla extract
1/4 tsp. lemon extract

Cream together margarine, butter, and cream cheese in a large bowl. Add 2 eggs, 1 cup flour, and 1 cup sugar; mix well. Repeat until all eggs, flour, and sugar have been added. Add extracts and mix well. Place batter in a greased and floured Bundt pan. Bake at 325°F for 1 hour and 15 minutes, or until a toothpick inserted in the center comes out clean.

Moist Lemon Cake

1 c. butter
1 c. sugar
4 eggs, beaten
1 c. self-rising flour, sifted
juice of 2 lemons
3 tbsp. confectioners' sugar

Cream butter and sugar. Add beaten eggs and sifted flour alternately. Turn into an 8 x 8-inch or 9 x 9-inch square or round pan. Bake at 400°F for 50 minutes.

Boil lemon juice and sugar. Remove cake from oven, and immediately pour boiling lemon mixture over it. Cool in pan.

Note: This recipe works well with most juices. Try orange, cranberry, or pineapple.

Fruit Upside Down Cake

4 tbsp. butter
1/2 c. light brown sugar
1/4 tsp. grated nutmeg
2 c. peaches, sliced thin
1 tsp. fresh lemon juice
1 1/3 c. cake flour
3/4 c. sugar
1 3/4 tsp. baking powder
1/4 tsp. salt
3 tbsp. butter, softened
1/2 c. milk
1 tsp. vanilla extract
1 egg

Melt the 4 tablespoons of butter in an 8-inch square pan. Add the brown sugar and nutmeg and blend well. Remove the pan from heat and arrange the peach slices, slightly overlapping them, on the brown sugar mixture. Sprinkle the peach slices with lemon juice.

Sift the flour with the sugar, baking powder, and salt. Stir the 3 tablespoons of butter to soften it, then stir in the flour mixture, milk, and vanilla extract. Mix until flour is dampened. Beat the batter for 2 minutes with an electric mixer at medium speed. Add egg, and beat for 1 minute longer. Pour batter over peaches.

Bake in a preheated oven at 375°F for 35 minutes. Cool in pan for 5 minutes, then invert cake on to a serving plate. Let stand for 1 minute more before removing the pan. Serve warm.

Apple Pie Cake

1/4 c. butter
1 c. sugar
1 egg
1/4 tsp. salt
1 tsp. cinnamon
1 tsp. nutmeg
1 tsp. baking soda
1 c. flour
1/2 c. chopped nuts
2 1/2 c. diced apples
1 tsp. vanilla extract
2 tbsp. hot water
whipped cream or ice cream

Combine ingredients in order given. (Batter will be thick). Bake in a greased 9-inch pie pan for 45 minutes at 350°F. Serve warm with whipped cream or ice cream.

Grammie's Banana Cake

2/3 c. shortening
2 1/2 c. sifted cake flour
1 2/3 c. sugar
1 1/4 tsp. baking powder
1 tsp. baking soda
1 tsp. salt
1 1/4 c. mashed, fully ripe bananas
2/3 c. buttermilk, divided
2 eggs
2/3 c. chopped walnuts

Place shortening in mixing bowl. Sift in dry ingredients. Add bananas and 1/3 cup buttermilk. Mix until moistened; beat 2 minutes at medium speed. Add remaining 1/3 cup buttermilk and eggs. Beat 2 minutes more. Fold in chopped walnuts. Bake in 2 greased and lightly floured 9-inch cake pans at 350°F for 35 minutes. Cool 10 minutes in pans, then remove from pans and cool completely.

Chocolate Chip Cake

Sift together:
2 1/2 c. flour
3 tsp. baking powder
1 tsp. baking soda
1/4 tsp. salt

Cream together:
1 c. butter or margarine
1 c. sugar
3 eggs

Add to the cream mixture:
1 c. sour cream
2 tsp. vanilla extract

Add flour mixture to creamed butter mixture.

Mix together the following:
1 c. chopped walnuts
1 c. chocolate chips
1/2 c. brown sugar
2 tsp. cinnamon

Grease a tube pan. Pour half of batter in the pan then sprinkle on half the chocolate chip mixture. Add remaining batter, then sprinkle with remaining chocolate chip mixture on top. Bake 1 hour at 350°F.

Amaretto Cheesecake

Hazelnut Crust and Macaroon Bits:

1 c. roasted hazelnuts (350°F for 10 minutes)
3 egg whites
2 tsp. vanilla extract
2 c. confectioners' sugar, divided
1/2 c. granulated sugar
1/8 tsp. salt
1/4 c. amaretto
Amaretto Cream Cheese Filling (recipe follows)

Heat oven to 350°F. Grease a 10-inch springform pan and line with greased parchment (not wax paper). Line a cookie sheet with greased parchment.

Whisk together egg whites and vanilla extract. Remove as much skin from the hazelnuts as possible and process them with 1 cup of confectioners' sugar for 30 seconds. Add remaining confectioners' sugar, granulated sugar, and salt; process briefly to combine. With processor running, pour in egg mixture and process for 15 seconds, or until smooth.

Reserve 1/2 to 1/3 cup of the batter. Pour remaining batter into prepared pan and smooth with spatula. Pour reserved batter on cookie sheet and spread into a 7–8 inch disk. Bake crust 25–30 minutes and disk 20–25 minutes. Cool on a wire rack. Chop up disk into 1/8-inch pieces and soak in 1/4 cup amaretto (but do not soak for more than 15 minutes).

Amaretto Cream Cheese Filling:

3 tsp. unflavored gelatin
1/4 c. amaretto
1 1/2 lb. cream cheese
2 tbsp. lemon juice
1 tsp. lemon zest
2 c. cream, divided
2 tsp. vanilla extract
3/4 c. sugar

Sprinkle gelatin over amaretto, let stand 5 minutes. Heat in saucepan with hot (not boiling) water, stirring for 4 minutes. Leave in hot water to stay warm. Beat cream cheese with mixer for 1 minute. Add lemon juice and zest. Beat cream to soft peaks. Fold one-third of cream into cream cheese. Fold in remaining whipped cream and soaked macaroon bits. Pour into prepared crust, cover with plastic wrap. Refrigerate at least 3 hours or preferably overnight.

Cocoa Cola Cake

2 c. flour
2 c. sugar
1 c. butter
2 tsp. cocoa
1 c. cola (do not use diet)
1/2 c. buttermilk
2 eggs, beaten
1 tsp. baking soda
1 tsp. vanilla extract
1 1/2 c. miniature marshmallows
Cocoa Cola Frosting (recipe follows)

Combine flour and sugar in a large bowl. Melt butter. Add cocoa and cola; heat to boiling. Cool slightly. Pour over flour mixture; mix well. Add buttermilk, beaten eggs, soda, and vanilla extract. Mix well and stir in marshmallows. Pour into greased and floured 13 x 9-inch pan. Bake at 350°F for 40 minutes. Frost while hot.

Cocoa Cola Frosting:

2 tbsp. butter
2 tbsp. cocoa
8 tbsp. cola (do not use diet)
2 c. confectioners' sugar
1 c. chopped nuts

Heat butter, cocoa, and cola to boiling. Add sugar and mix well. Stir in chopped nuts.

Becky's Walnut Cake

2 c. flour
2 c. sugar
1 (8-oz.) can crushed pineapple
2 eggs
2 tsp. soda
1 tsp. vanilla extract
2 c. crushed walnuts, divided
Walnut Icing (recipe follows)

Preheat oven to 350°F. Mix together all ingredients except nuts. Be sure to use the whole can of pineapple, including liquid. Mix by hand, or use mixer on medium speed until thoroughly mixed. Add 1 1/2 cups of nuts. Pour batter into a greased and floured 9 x 13-inch pan and bake for 45 minutes. Allow cake to cool at least 20 minutes, then remove from pan.

Walnut Icing:
2 c. confectioners' sugar
1 stick butter, softened
1 (8-oz.) pkg. cream cheese, softened
reserved 1/2 cup walnuts

Using mixer, blend all ingredients together except walnuts. Icing should be very creamy. Spread over top and sides of cake. Sprinkle reserved walnuts on top.

Bailey's Chocolate Chip Cheesecake

Crust:
2 c. graham cracker crumbs
1/4 c. sugar
6 tbsp. butter, melted

Preheat oven to 325°F. Coat 9-inch springform pan with nonstick vegetable oil spray. Combine crumbs and sugar in pan. Stir in butter. Press mixture into bottom and 1 inch up sides of pan. Bake until light brown, about 7 minutes.

Filling:
2 1/4 lb. cream cheese, room temperature
1 2/3 c. sugar
5 eggs, room temperature
1 c. Bailey's Irish Cream
1 tbsp. vanilla extract
1 c. semi-sweet chocolate chips, divided

Using electric mixer, beat cream cheese until smooth. Gradually mix in sugar. Beat in eggs, one at a time. Blend in Bailey's and vanilla extract. Sprinkle half of chocolate chips over crust. Spoon in filling. Sprinkle with remaining chocolate chips. Bake cake until puffed, springy in center, and golden brown, about 1 hour and 20 minutes. Cool cake completely.

Coffee Cream:
1 c. chilled whipping cream
2 tbsp. sugar
1 tsp. instant coffee powder
chocolate curls

Beat cream, sugar, and coffee powder until peaks form. Spread mixture over cooled cake. Garnish cake with chocolate curls.

Taylor's Basic Cheesecake

1 c. graham cracker crumbs
3 tbsp. sugar
3 tbsp. butter or margarine, melted
4 (8 oz.) pkgs. cream cheese, softened
1 c. sugar
3 tbsp. flour
4 eggs
1 c. sour cream
1 tbsp. vanilla extract

Heat oven to 350°F. For crust, mix crumbs, 3 tablespoons sugar, and butter. Press into bottom of a 9-inch springform pan. Bake 10 minutes.

For filling, beat cream cheese, 1 cup sugar, and flour at medium speed with mixer until well blended. Add eggs, one at a time, mixing well after each addition. Blend in sour cream and vanilla extract. Pour over prepared crust.

Bake 1 hour and 10 minutes.

Turn off oven and prop door open. Let cheesecake sit in oven until oven has cooled. Loosen cake from rim of pan.

Note: Cake can be topped with fruits or whipped cream as desired. It tastes best when refrigerated overnight.

Annie's Aloha Cake

1 box yellow cake mix
1 c. crushed pineapple, undrained
1/2 c. sugar
1 (3-oz.) pkg. instant vanilla pudding
1 c. coconut, shredded
8 oz. whipped topping, thawed
1 c. pecans, toasted and chopped

Bake cake according to directions in a 9 x 13-inch pan. In a saucepan over medium heat, combine pineapple with juice, sugar, pudding, and coconut. Simmer 5 minutes. Using a wooden spoon handle, poke holes in warm cake. Slowly pour pineapple mixture over cake and spread evenly. Cool. Spread whipped topping evenly over cake and sprinkle with nuts. Chill at least 2 hours before serving.

Big Slice of Heaven Cake

1 box yellow cake mix
1 (3 1/2-oz.) pkg. instant vanilla pudding
1 c. sour cream
1 c. milk
1/2 c. vegetable oil
1 stick butter, softened
4 eggs
1 (6-oz.) pkg. chocolate pieces
1 oz. German sweet chocolate, grated
1 c. chopped pecans
1 (8-oz.) pkg. soft cream cheese
1 lb. confectioners' sugar
1 tsp. vanilla extract
1 c. chopped nuts
1 1/3 c. coconut

Mix first 7 ingredients for 2 minutes at medium speed. Stir in chocolate pieces, grated chocolate, and 1 cup pecans. Pour in greased and floured Bundt pan. Bake at 350°F for 1 hour, or until toothpick comes out clean. Cool in pan for 25 minutes. Turn and cool completely.

For frosting, beat cream cheese until light and fluffy. Beat in confectioners' sugar and vanilla extract. Stir in nuts and coconut. Frost the cooled cake.

Black Walnut Carrot Cake

3 c. grated carrots
4 eggs
1 1/2 c. oil
2 c. sugar
2 c. sifted flour
1 c. chopped black walnuts
1 tsp. vanilla extract
1/4 tsp. black walnut extract
1 tsp. cinnamon
Buttermilk Glaze (recipe follows)

Preheat oven to 350°F. Grease a 10-inch tube pan. Mix together all ingredients. Bake 90 minutes. Remove from oven and, while cake is still hot, pour Buttermilk Glaze over cake.

Buttermilk Glaze:
1/2 c. buttermilk
1 c. sifted confectioners' sugar
1/2 tsp. baking soda
1 tbsp. white corn syrup

Blend well and pour on top of hot cake. Let stand for 1 hour. Remove cake from pan and serve.

Blueberry Ice Box Cake

Crust:
2 c. graham cracker crumbs
1/2 c. confectioners' sugar
1/2 c. butter

Mix crust ingredients well and spread evenly in a 9 x 13-inch pan.

Cream Filling:
1 (8-oz.) pkg. cream cheese
3 eggs, beaten
1 c. sugar

Cream together all ingredients and spread over crumb mixture. Bake 30 minutes at 350°F.

Topping:
juice of 1/2 lemon
1 can blueberry pie filling

Mix lemon juice and pie filling together well. Pour over cream filling while still hot. When completely cool, cover entire cake with whipped topping. Keeps very well in the refrigerator.

Blueberry Muffin Cake

4 oz. plain whole wheat flour
8 oz. plain white flour
1/8 tsp. salt
1 tsp. baking powder
grated rind of 1 orange
6 oz. light brown sugar
8 oz. blueberries
2 eggs
1/2 c. milk
1 oz. melted butter
milk to glaze
confectioners' sugar

Preheat oven to 425°F. Sift together flours, salt, and baking powder. Stir in orange rind, sugar, and blueberries. Whisk together eggs, milk, and butter. Stir the liquid mixture into the dry mixture and blend well. Pour into greased cake pan. Bake above the center of the oven for 35 minutes. Remove cake from oven, glaze with milk, and sprinkle with confectioners' sugar. Return to oven to bake for an additional 5 minutes. Serve warm or cold.

Note: You can also make muffins with this recipe. Reduce baking time to 20 minutes.

Carrot Cake with Bourbon Glaze

2/3 c. oil
1 c. sugar
2 eggs
1 c. flour
1 tsp. baking powder
1 tsp. baking soda
1/2 tsp. salt
1/2 tsp. cinnamon
1/4 tsp. nutmeg
3 tbsp. bourbon
1 1/2 c. grated carrots
1 c. chopped pecans
Bourbon Glaze (recipe follows)

Beat oil and sugar together until well mixed. Beat in eggs. Then add flour, baking powder, soda, salt, cinnamon, and nutmeg; mix well. Add bourbon, carrots, and pecans. Pour into greased and floured 9 x 9-inch cake pan. Bake at 325°F for 40 minutes. Cool in pan before spreading Bourbon Glaze over cake.

Bourbon Glaze:
1 c. confectioners' sugar
2 tbsp. hot water
1 tbsp. bourbon

Blend together and spread over cooled cake.

Brown Sugar Carrot Cake

2 c. flour
2 c. brown sugar
2 tsp. baking powder
2 tsp. baking soda
1 1/2 tsp. cinnamon
1/2 tsp. salt
1 c. oil
4 eggs
3 c. grated carrots
1 c. chopped pecans or walnuts

In large bowl, mix together flour, brown sugar, baking powder, soda, cinnamon, and salt. Add oil to mixture and then eggs, one at a time, beating thoroughly after each addition. Blend in carrots and nuts. Pour into greased 9 x 13-inch baking pan. Bake at 350°F for 45 minutes.

Buttermilk Spice Cake

2 1/2 c. all-purpose flour
1 tsp. baking powder
1 tsp. soda
1 tsp. salt
1 c. granulated sugar
3/4 c. brown sugar, packed
3/4 tsp. cinnamon
3/4 tsp. allspice
1/2 tsp. cloves
1/2 tsp. nutmeg
1 1/3 c. buttermilk
1/2 c. shortening
3 eggs

Grease and flour 2 round layer pans, 8- or 9-inch. Measure all ingredients into large mixing bowl. Blend 2 minutes on low speed, scraping bowl occasionally. Pour into pans. Bake in preheated 350°F oven for 45 minutes, or until wooden toothpick inserted into center comes out clean. Cool 10 minutes and remove from pans. Wonderful with a lemon or chocolate frosting.

Carrot and Cranberry Cake

3 c. sifted flour
2 tsp. baking powder
1 tsp. baking soda
1/2 tsp. salt
1/2 tsp. cinnamon
1/2 tsp. nutmeg
1/2 tsp. ground cloves
1 c. light brown sugar, packed
1 c. sugar
1 c. oil
4 eggs, beaten
1 c. whole cranberry sauce
1 c. grated carrots
1/2 c. candied lemon peel, chopped

In a mixing bowl, sift together flour, baking powder, soda, salt, cinnamon, nutmeg, and cloves. Add sugars, oil, beaten eggs, and cranberry sauce. Mix well, and then stir in carrots and lemon peel. Pour into greased and floured tube pan. Bake at 350°F for 90 minutes, or until cake springs back when lightly touched.

Aunt Lena's Carrot Cake

1 1/2 c. flour
1 tsp. baking powder
1 1/4 c. brown sugar
2 tsp. cinnamon
3/4 tsp. cardamom
1/8 tsp. ground cloves
1 pinch salt

1 c. finely grated carrots
1 lemon, peel and juice
1 c. ground almonds
4 eggs, beaten
1 c. melted and cooled margarine
marzipan carrots (optional)

Mix together flour and baking powder and sift. Add sugar, cinnamon, cardamom, cloves, and salt to flour mixture. Add carrots, grated lemon peel, juice, and almonds. Finally, add beaten eggs and margarine.

Stir with a wooden spatula until smooth. Pour into a greased loaf pan and cook for about 65 minutes on the lowest rack of the oven, preheated to 350°F. After 50 minutes, "plant" little marzipan carrots in a row on top of the cake. Remove from oven and allow to cool.

Fruity Pie Cake

2 cans prepared pie filling in your favorite flavor (apple, cherry, peach, etc.)
1 box yellow or white cake mix (2-layer size)
1/2 c. butter
1/2 c. pecans or walnuts
1 tsp. cinnamon or nutmeg

Grease a 13 x 9-inch pan. Place filling in pan. Sprinkle cake mix evenly over filling. Melt butter and pour over cake mix. Sprinkle nuts over everything, then sprinkle spice over that. Bake at 350°F for about 35–45 minutes.

Serve warm with ice cream.

Big Orange Cake

1 c. butter
1 1/2 c. sugar
4 eggs
3 c. white flour
1 tsp. baking soda
1/2 c. orange juice
1 c. chopped walnuts
1 c. flaked coconut
8 oz. chopped dates

Glaze:
1/2 c. orange juice
1 c. confectioners' sugar

Grease and lightly flour two 9 x 5 x 3-inch loaf pans. Preheat oven to 300°F. In a large bowl, cream butter and gradually beat in sugar. Add eggs, one at a time, and beat well after each addition.

Sift together flour and baking soda. Stir flour mixture into butter mixture in three parts, alternating with the orange juice. Mix nuts, coconut, and dates; fold gently into batter. Pour batter into greased pans and bake for 60–90 minutes, or until golden brown. For glaze, mix together orange juice and confectioners' sugar. Pour over cakes in pans while still hot. Cool in pans on racks. Makes two loaves.

Light Fruit Cake

1 1/2 c. butter, softened
1 1/2 c. sugar
1 tbsp. vanilla extract
7 eggs, separated
3 c. all-purpose flour
1 1/2 lb. diced yellow, green, and
  red candied pineapple
1 lb. red and green candied cherries
1/4 lb. diced candied citron
1/2 lb. golden raisins
3 c. pecan halves
1 c. black walnuts, coarsely chopped
1/2 c. all-purpose flour
additional candied fruit and nuts (optional)
1/4 c. brandy

Make a liner for a 10-inch tube-pan by drawing a circle with an 18-inch diameter on a piece of brown paper. Cut out circle, set pan in center, and draw around base of pan and inside tube. Fold circle into eighths, having the drawn lines on the outside. Cut off tip end of circle along inside drawn line. Unfold paper; cut along folds to the outside drawn line. From another piece of brown paper, cut another circle with a 10-inch diameter; grease and set aside. Place the 18-inch liner in pan; grease and set aside.

Cream butter; gradually add sugar, beating well at medium speed with an electric mixer. Stir in vanilla. Beat egg yolks; alternately add yolks and 3 cups flour to creamed mixture.

Combine candied pineapple, cherries, citron, raisins, pecans, and walnuts. Dredge with 1/2 cup flour, stirring to coat well. Stir mixture into batter. Beat egg whites until stiff peaks form; fold into batter.

Spoon batter into prepared pan. Arrange additional candied fruit and nuts on top of batter, if desired. Cover pan with 10-inch brown paper circle, greased side down. Bake at 250°F for about 4 hours, or until cake tests done. Remove from oven. Take off paper cover, and slowly pour 1/4 cup brandy evenly over cake; cool completely on wire rack.

Remove cake from pan; peel paper liner from cake. Wrap cake in brandy-soaked cheesecloth. Store in an airtight container in a cool place up to 3 weeks; pour a small amount of brandy over cake each week. Makes one 10-inch cake.

Rum Cake

1/3 c. chopped pecans
1 box yellow cake mix
3 eggs
1/2 c. vegetable oil
1/2 c. white or golden rum
1/2 c. water
1 small pkg. instant vanilla pudding
Rum Cake Glaze (recipe follows)

Heavily grease and flour a Bundt pan. Sprinkle nuts on bottom of pan. Mix all remaining ingredients, except glaze, and pour into pan over nuts. Bake at 325°F for 50–60 minutes.

While the cake is baking, make the Rum Cake Glaze. The glaze should be ready at the same time the cake is done.

Rum Cake Glaze:
1 stick butter
1/4 c. rum
1 c. sugar

Put glaze ingredients in a small pan and heat until boiling. Let boil for 2 minutes, no longer.

Pour glaze around outside of cake pan immediately upon removing from oven and cool in pan for 20 minutes.

Remove from pan and cool thoroughly.

Chocolate Chip Rum Cake

1 box yellow cake mix
1 (6-oz.) pkg. instant chocolate pudding
4 eggs
1 c. sour cream
1/2 c. oil
1 (12-oz.) bag semi-sweet chocolate morsels
1 tsp. vanilla extract
6–8 tbsp. rum

Mix all ingredients for 12 minutes at high speed. Bake in Bundt pan at 350°F for approximately 1 hour. Cool and invert on to cake platter.

Apple Cake

6 tbsp. sugar
1 tbsp. cinnamon
1 tbsp. baking powder
6 apples, peeled and sliced
1 tbsp. vanilla extract
4 eggs
1 c. oil
2 c. sugar
3 c. flour

Mix 6 tablespoons sugar, cinnamon, and baking powder in small bowl. Mix with apples. Add vanilla extract. Set aside.

In a separate bowl, beat eggs. Blend in oil. Gradually add sugar. Stir in flour until blended. Fold in apple mixture. Pour into greased Bundt pan. Bake at 375°F for 1 hour and 15 minutes, or until toothpick inserted in center comes out clean.

Savannah Cream Cake

1 envelope (1/4 oz.) unflavored gelatin
1/2 c. cold water
5 extra large egg yolks
1 c. sugar, divided
1/2 c. dry sherry
1/4 c. water
2 3/4 c. heavy cream, chilled, divided
1 tbsp. vanilla extract
1 Angel Food Cake, cut into 1-inch squares
   (recipe follows)
1 c. fresh strawberries, sliced
1 1/2 c. fresh raspberries, divided
1 1/2 tbsp. fresh lemon juice

In a small bowl, sprinkle gelatin into 1/2 cup cold water and let soften.

In a medium bowl, beat egg yolks and 1/2 cup sugar until thick and pale yellow, about 2 minutes. Stir in sherry and 1/4 cup water. Scrape egg yolk mixture into a heavy, medium-sized saucepan. Cook over moderate heat, stirring constantly, until custard thickens enough to coat the back of a spoon lightly; do not boil. Strain custard into a large bowl and whisk in the softened gelatin; set aside.

In a large bowl, whip 2 cups cream until it begins to thicken. Gradually beat in 1/4 cup sugar and vanilla extract. Beat until moderately stiff. Cover and refrigerate.

Set the bowl containing the custard and gelatin into a large bowl of ice and water. Whisk gently until custard is cold and beginning to set, 3–4 minutes. Remove from ice and fold in the whipped cream.

Fold the Angel Food Cake squares into the custard cream until they are completely coated. Spoon this mixture into a buttered 10-inch tube pan. Cover and refrigerate until set, 1 to 2 hours.

In a food processor, combine strawberries, 1 cup raspberries, remaining sugar, and lemon juice; purée until smooth. Strain if desired to remove the seeds. Cover and refrigerate until chilled. Beat the remaining 3/4 cup cream until moderately stiff.

To unmold the cake, wrap the tube pan briefly in a hot wet towel and run a knife around the edge. Unmold the cake on to a platter and cover with the whipped cream. Garnish with the remaining 1/2 cup raspberries and serve the strawberry-raspberry sauce on the side.

Angel Food Cake:
1 c. plus 2 tbsp. cake flour
1/4 tsp. grated nutmeg
1 1/2 c. sugar, divided
12 extra large egg whites
1 1/4 tsp. cream of tartar
1/2 tsp. salt
1 tsp. vanilla extract

Preheat oven to 375° F. Sift together the flour, nutmeg, and 1/2 cup sugar.

In a large bowl, beat egg whites until frothy. Add cream of tartar and salt. Gradually beat in the remaining sugar, a tablespoon at a time, until stiff, shiny peaks form. Beat in the vanilla extract and fold in the flour mixture.

Turn batter into an ungreased 10-inch tube pan. Bake for 30 minutes, or until a toothpick comes out clean. Invert on a rack to cool.

Black Forest Cheesecake

Cherry Topping:
1 lb. frozen unsweetened cherries, thawed
1/4 c. kirsch
1/4 c. cherry syrup or sour cherry syrup

Soak undrained cherries and kirsch in small bowl for 6 hours. Thoroughly drain cherries in strainer set over medium bowl, shaking occasionally, for at least 2 hours. Reserve liquid.

Add enough cherry syrup to cherry liquid to measure 1 cup. Pour 6 tablespoons into a heavy, 8-inch skillet (reserve remaining liquid for filling). Halve cherries and add to skillet. Boil until syrup is thickened and mixture resembles preserves, about 6 minutes. Chill. (Can be prepared ahead.)

Chocolate Crust:
8 1/2 oz. chocolate wafer cookies
6 tbsp. well-chilled butter, cut into
　 1/2-inch pieces

Generously butter a 9-inch springform pan. Finely crush cookies in processor. Cut in butter until mixture begins to gather together. Press crumbs into bottom of pan and up sides to within 3/4 inch from top. Refrigerate crust for at least 30 minutes.

Chocolate Filling:
1 1/2 c. whipping cream
12 oz. semi-sweet chocolate, coarsely chopped
16 oz. cream cheese, room temperature

3/4 c. sugar
4 eggs, room temperature
10 tbsp. cherry liquid (from Cherry Topping)
1 tsp. vanilla extract
1 c. whipping cream, well-chilled
2 tbsp. sugar
1 tbsp. kirsch
chocolate curls

Preheat oven to 325°F. Heat 1 1/2 cups whipping cream with chocolate in heavy saucepan over low heat, stirring constantly, until chocolate melts. Cool 10 minutes.

Beat cream cheese with 3/4 cup sugar until smooth.

Beat in eggs, one at a time, until just combined.

Beat in chocolate mixture, then remaining 10 tablespoons cherry liquid, and vanilla extract. Pour into crust.

Bake until outer 2 inches of cake are firm but center still moves slightly, about 1 hour and 15 minutes (top may crack).

Cool completely on rack. Top pan with paper towels and cover tightly with foil. Refrigerate 1 to 2 days. Remove foil, paper towels, and pan sides from cake. Spread cherry topping over cake.

Beat remaining 1 cup whipping cream with 2 tablespoons sugar, and kirsch to peaks. Spoon on to center of cake. Top with chocolate curls if desired. (Can be prepared up to 2 hours ahead and refrigerated.) Let stand at room temperature for 15 minutes before serving.

Supreme Cheesecake

3/4 c. plus 2 tbsp. all-purpose flour, divided
3 tbsp. sugar
1 tsp. grated lemon peel, divided
6 tbsp. butter
1 egg yolk, slightly beaten
1/2 tsp. vanilla extract, divided
3 (8-oz.) pkgs. cream cheese, softened
1 c. sugar
1/4 tsp. salt
2 eggs
1 egg yolk
1/4 c. milk
Cherry Sauce (recipe follows)

To prepare crust, combine 3/4 cup flour, 3 tablespoons sugar, and 1/2 teaspoon lemon peel. Cut in butter until crumbly. Stir in 1 slightly beaten egg yolk and 1/4 teaspoon vanilla extract. Pat one-third of dough on to the bottom of an 8- or 9-inch springform pan (with sides removed). Bake in a 400°F oven for 7 minutes, or until golden brown. Cool.

Butter the sides of pan; attach to bottom. Pat remaining dough on to sides of pan to a height of 1 3/4 inches; set aside.

In a large bowl beat together the softened cream cheese, remaining lemon peel, and remaining vanilla extract until fluffy.

Stir together 1 cup sugar, 2 tablespoons flour, and salt; then gradually stir this into cream cheese mixture. Add the 2 eggs and 1 egg yolk all at once, beating at low speed just until combined. Stir in milk.

Turn into crust-lined pan. Bake in a 450°F oven for 10 minutes. Reduce heat to 300°F and bake 50–55 minutes, or until center appears set and a knife comes out clean. Cool 15 minutes. Loosen sides of cheesecake from pan with a spatula. Cool 30 minutes; remove sides of pan. Cool about 2 hours longer. Chill thoroughly. Top with Cherry Sauce.

Cherry Sauce:
3/4 c. sugar
2 tbsp. cornstarch
dash of salt
1/3 c. water
4 c. unsweetened red cherries, pitted, fresh or frozen

In a saucepan combine sugar, cornstarch, and salt. Stir in water and thawed cherries. Cook and stir until thickened and bubbly. Cook and stir 1–2 minutes more. Cover. Chill without stirring.

Cinnamon Breakfast Cake

2 c. flour, sifted
4 tsp. baking powder
1/2 tsp. salt
4 tbsp. brown sugar
4 tbsp. solid shortening
1 egg, well beaten
1/2 c. milk
1/4 c. seedless raisins
1 tbsp. butter, melted
2 tbsp. sugar
1 tsp. cinnamon

Sift flour with baking powder and salt. Add brown sugar. Cut in shortening and add egg along with milk to form a soft dough. Add raisins. Spread in well-oiled and floured cake pan. Pour melted butter over top of cake. Sprinkle with sugar and cinnamon. Bake in hot oven at 425° F for 20–30 minutes.

Prune Cake

Cake:

1 c. vegetable oil
1 1/2 c. sugar
1 c. buttermilk
2 c. all-purpose flour
3 eggs
2 tsp. baking powder
1 tsp. salt
1 tsp. cinnamon
1 tsp. nutmeg
1 tsp. baking soda
1/2 tsp. allspice
2 tsp. vanilla extract
1 tsp. lemon extract
1 c. chopped, pitted prunes
1 c. chopped pecans

Sauce:

1/2 c. sugar
1/4 c. buttermilk
1 tbsp. light corn syrup
1/2 stick butter, cut into pieces
1/4 tsp. baking soda
1/2 tsp. vanilla extract
1/2 tsp. lemon extract

Preheat oven to 350° F. Make cake by mixing all ingredients. Pour into a greased and floured tube pan. Bake until cake tests done, about 1 hour. Let cool in pan about 10 minutes; turn out on rack and cool completely.

For sauce, combine all ingredients in a large saucepan. Bring to a boil and continue boiling until mixture will spin a thread when poured off the end of a spoon, about 10 minutes. Cool slightly. Poke holes through cooled cake with a skewer and pour half of sauce over top. Wrap tightly and let sit for two to 2–3 days before serving. Serve with remaining sauce on the side.

Spicy Pineapple Zucchini Cake

Cake:

4 eggs
1 c. vegetable oil
2 c. sugar
2 tsp. vanilla extract
2 c. grated zucchini
8 oz. pineapple, crushed and drained
2 tsp. baking soda
1 tsp. salt
1 tsp. baking powder
1 1/2 tsp. cinnamon
3/4 tsp. ground nutmeg
1 c. walnuts
3 c. flour
1 c. raisins

Frosting:

3 oz. cream cheese
1/4 tsp. lemon flavoring
1/2 tsp. almond flavoring
8 oz. confectioners' sugar
4 tbsp. butter

For cake, beat eggs to blend. Add oil, sugar, and vanilla. Continue beating until thick and foamy. Stir in zucchini and pineapple.

Mix remaining ingredients in a separate bowl. Stir dry mixture into zucchini mixture just until blended. Bake in preheated oven at 350° F for 1 hour, or until toothpick inserted in center comes out clean. Top with frosting.

Frosting:

Cream ingredients, beating until smooth. Spread over cooled cake.

Banana Split Cake

Crust #1:
2 c. graham cracker crumbs
1/4 c. butter

Crust #2:
2 c. flour
1/2 c. sugar
1 c butter, softened
1 egg, slightly beaten
1/2 tsp. vanilla

Crust #3:
32 chocolate sandwich cookies
2/3 c. butter, melted

Filling:
1/2 c. butter
2 1/2 c. confectioners' sugar
2 eggs, blended
5 bananas, sliced lengthwise
20 oz. pineapple chunks, drained
4 c. whole strawberries
1 c. whipping cream
1/2 c. chopped walnuts

Mix ingredients for first crust and press in the bottom of a 9 x 13-inch pan. Bake 10 minutes at 350° F. Cool.

Blend all ingredients for second crust thoroughly. Pat dough on top of cooled first crust. Bake at 400° F for about 10 minutes, or until golden brown. Cool.

For third crust, crush cookies and mix them with the butter. Press mixture over cooled second crust. Cool. For the filling, whip butter, sugar, and eggs with electric mixer and spread over cooled crust. Place bananas, cut side down, on top of butter layer. Spread on the pineapple chunks, then the strawberries. Whip the cream. Cover the entire dish with whipped cream, and sprinkle with nuts. Refrigerate for 4 hours before serving.

Blackberry Jam Cake

1/2 c. sugar
1/4 c. butter
2 eggs
1 c. all-purpose flour
1/2 tsp. baking soda
1/4 tsp. ground cloves
1/4 tsp. ground nutmeg
1 tsp. ground cinnamon
1/3 c. buttermilk
1/2 c. seedless blackberry jam
1/4 c. chopped walnuts

Icing:
2 tbsp. butter
1/2 c. brown sugar, packed
3 tbsp. milk
1 3/4 c. confectioners' sugar, sifted

Cream together sugar and butter. Beat in eggs. Stir together flour, baking soda, and spices. Add to creamed mixture alternately with buttermilk, beating until well blended after each addition. Fold in blackberry jam and nuts leaving swirls of jam. Do not over mix. Turn into greased and lightly floured 9 x 9 x 2-inch baking pan. Bake at 350° F for 25 minutes, or until done. Cool completely.

For icing, in a small saucepan, melt butter and stir in brown sugar. Cook, stirring constantly, until mixture bubbles; remove from heat. Cool 5 minutes. Stir in milk and confectioners' sugar. Beat until spreading consistency is reached.

Cookies

Grease:
To apply a thin layer of butter, shortening, or oil to a pan or other equipment to prevent foods from sticking.

Knead:
To work dough into a uniform mixture by pressing, folding, stretching, and turning.

Zest:
To remove the outmost skin of citrus fruit with a knife, peeler, or zester.

Snickerdoodles

1 c. shortening
1 1/2 c. sugar
2 eggs
2 3/4 c. flour
2 tsp. cream of tartar
1 tsp. baking soda
1/4 tsp. salt
1/2 c. sugar
1/2 c. cinnamon

Mix together thoroughly the shortening, 1 1/2 cups sugar, and eggs. Sift together the flour, cream of tartar, soda, and salt. Stir the two mixtures together. Roll the dough into balls the size of walnuts. Dip in mixture of equal parts cinnamon and sugar. Place 2 inches apart on lightly greased baking sheet. Bake until lightly browned but still soft (8–10 minutes) at 400°F.

Makes 3 dozen.

Chocolate Chip Oatmeal Cookies

1 c. shortening
3/4 c. granulated sugar
3/4 c. light brown sugar
2 eggs, beaten
1 tsp. vanilla extract
1 3/4 c. flour
1/2 tsp. salt
1 tsp. baking soda
2/3 c. quick cooking oatmeal
1 c. pecans
1 (6-oz.) pkg. chocolate chips

Cream together shortening and sugars. Add 2 beaten eggs and vanilla. Sift together flour, salt, and baking soda. Add to creamed mixture, blending well. Add oatmeal, nuts, and chocolate chips. Drop by teaspoonfuls on to baking sheet. Bake at 350°F for 12–15 minutes.

Note: Try this recipe with butterscotch chips and walnuts.

Praline Cookies

1 1/2 c. flour
1 1/2 c. brown sugar
1 1/2 tsp. baking powder
1/2 tsp. salt
2/3 c. solid shortening
1 tsp. vanilla
1 egg
1/2 c. chopped pecans
Brown Sugar Glaze (recipe follows)

Preheat oven to 350°F. In a large bowl, combine all ingredients except pecans and glaze. Blend at medium speed to form stiff dough. Drop by teaspoonfuls on ungreased cookie sheets. Bake 10–13 minutes until deep, golden brown. Cool. Top each cookie with 1/2 teaspoon pecans. Drizzle with Brown Sugar Glaze.

Brown Sugar Glaze:
2 tbsp. butter
1/4 c. brown sugar
1 1/2 to 2 1/2 tbsp. milk
3/4 c. confectioners' sugar

In small saucepan, melt butter. Stir in brown sugar and milk. Add confectioners' sugar; blend to make a glazing consistency.

Makes 4 dozen cookies.

Butter Spritz

2 c. butter
1 1/2 c. sugar
2 eggs or 6 yolks
1 tsp. almond extract
1 tsp. vanilla extract
5 c. flour
1 tsp. baking powder
1/4 tsp. salt

Cream butter and sugar. Add eggs. Add extracts. Sift together flour, baking powder, and salt. Add to mixture. Batter will be very stiff. Use cookie press and bake at 350°F for 8 minutes, or until golden brown.

Note: You may refrigerate the dough to make it less sticky and even refrigerate the cookie sheets between batches to help the cookies stick to the sheet instead of melting on a hot cookie sheet.

Chocolate Almond Macaroons

Cookies:
1 c. semi-sweet chocolate chips
2 egg whites
8 oz. almond paste
1/3 c. sifted confectioners' sugar
2 tbsp. all-purpose flour

Preheat oven to 300°F. In top of double boiler, melt chocolate chips, stirring until smooth. Set aside.

In large bowl, combine egg whites, almond paste, confectioners' sugar, and flour; beat until smooth. Blend in melted chocolate.

Spoon macaroon mixture into pastry bag fitted with rosette tip. Pipe 1 3/4-inch rosettes on to foil-lined cookie sheets. Bake for 25 minutes. Cool completely on wire racks.

Topping:
1 c. semi-sweet chocolate chips, divided
1 tbsp. vegetable shortening
1/4 c. chopped blanched almonds

Combine 3/4 cup chocolate chips and vegetable shortening over hot (*not* boiling) water in top of double boiler. Stir until morsels are melted and mixture is smooth. Drizzle each macaroon with 1/2 teaspoonful of chocolate. Sprinkle with remaining 1/4 cup chocolate chips and chopped almonds.

Chocolate Macaroons

2 c. shredded coconut
1/3 c. sugar
1 tbsp. light corn syrup
2 tbsp. flour
3 tbsp. cocoa
1 tsp. vanilla extract
2 egg whites, unbeaten
dash of salt

Preheat oven to 325°F. In a medium bowl, mix together coconut, sugar, corn syrup, flour, and cocoa until well blended. Stir in vanilla extract, unbeaten egg whites, and salt. Mix well.

Using a small ice cream scoop, place 15 small mounds of coconut mixture on a greased, foil-lined cookie sheet, 1 1/2 inches apart.

Bake 18–22 minutes until just set. Let cool in pan. When cool, carefully separate cookies from foil.

Oatmeal Chocolate Cookies

1/2 c. milk
2 c. sugar
1/4 c. cocoa
1 stick butter
3 c. oatmeal
1 tsp. vanilla extract
1/4 c. peanut butter (optional)

Combine milk, sugar, cocoa, and butter. Cook over medium heat while stirring until mixture boils. Let boil for 5 minutes, then remove from heat. Immediately stir in oatmeal, vanilla extract, and peanut butter.

Drop by heaping teaspoonfuls on wax paper and let cool.

Chocolate Peanut Butter Cookies

1 1/2 c. brown sugar, firmly packed
1 c. chunky peanut butter
3/4 c. margarine
1/3 c. water
1 egg
1 tsp. vanilla extract
3 c. oats
1 1/2 c. flour
1/2 tsp. baking soda
1 c. sugar
1 1/2 c. semi-sweet chocolate chips
4 tsp. vegetable shortening
1/3 c. chopped peanuts

Preheat oven to 350°F. Beat brown sugar, peanut butter, and margarine until fluffy. Blend in water, egg, and vanilla extract. Combine oats, flour, and baking soda; add to mixture. Mix well. Cover and chill 1 hour.

Shape into 1-inch balls and place on ungreased cookie sheet. Using the bottom of a glass dipped into sugar, press into 1/4-inch thick circles. Bake 8–10 minutes, or until edges are golden brown. Cool on wire rack.

Melt chocolate pieces as package directs. Stir in vegetable shortening, mixing until smooth. Top each cookie with 1/2 teaspoon of melted chocolate. Sprinkle with chopped peanuts.

Coconut Macaroons

3 pkgs. flaked coconut
1 can sweetened condensed milk
2 tsp. vanilla
1 1/2 tsp. almond extract

Preheat oven to 325°F. In large mixing bowl combine all ingredients; mix well.

Drop by rounded spoonfuls on to well-greased cookie sheets.

Bake on middle rack of oven, 12 at a time, for 10–12 minutes, or until browned around edges.

Cool slightly.

Remove to wire racks; cool completely. Store loosely covered at room temperature.

Makes about 4 dozen.

Variation: Omit almond extract. Add 4 squares unsweetened chocolate (melted) or 1 cup of chocolate chips. Proceed as above.

Texas Cookies

1/2 lb. butter
1 c. sugar
1 c. dark brown sugar, packed
2 eggs
2 c. flour
1 tsp. salt
1 tsp. baking soda
1/2 tsp. baking powder
3 c. rolled oats
1 (12-oz.) pkg. chocolate chips
1 tsp. vanilla extract

Preheat oven to 350°F. Mix butter, sugars, and eggs together in a large bowl.

In another bowl, mix flour, salt, soda, and baking powder. Blend both mixtures together thoroughly. Add oats, chocolate chips, and vanilla extract; mix well. Dough should be stiff but a bit sticky. Refrigerate for 1 hour.

Form dough into golf ball-sized balls and place on cookie sheet, spaced a little over 1 inch apart. Bake for 12–15 minutes. Cookies should be just brown on top, with golden brown bottoms and about 1/2 inch thick.

Peanut Butter Cookies

1/2 c. shortening
1/2 c. peanut butter
1/2 c. sugar
1/2 c. brown sugar
1 extra large egg
1 1/4 c. sifted flour
1/2 tsp. baking soda
1/2 tsp. baking powder
1/4 tsp. salt

Cream shortening and peanut butter until blended. Gradually add sugars, and beat until fluffy. Add egg, and beat thoroughly. Sift remaining ingredients together. Divide in half and add to creamed mixture, one half at a time, mixing until well blended after each addition.

Shape dough into 1 1/4-inch balls and place 3 inches apart on lightly greased cookie sheets. Flatten with fork, making a crisscross pattern. Bake at 375°F for about 10 minutes.

Amaretto Cheesecake Cookies

1 c. all-purpose flour
1/3 c. brown sugar, firmly packed
6 tbsp. butter, softened
8 oz. cream cheese, softened
1/4 c. granulated sugar
1 egg
4 tbsp. amaretto
1/2 tsp. vanilla extract
4 tbsp. chopped almonds

Preheat the oven to 350°F.

In a large mixing bowl, combine flour and brown sugar. Cut in butter until the mixture forms fine crumbs. Reserve 1 cup of the crumb mixture for the topping.

Press the remaining crumb mixture into the bottom of an ungreased, 8-inch square baking pan.

Bake for 12–15 minutes, or until lightly browned.

In a separate bowl, cream together the cheese and granulated sugar. Add the egg, amaretto, and vanilla extract; beating well. Spread the batter over the prepared crust.

Combine the almonds with the reserved crumb mixture. Sprinkle over the batter.

Bake for 20–25 minutes. Cool and cut into squares.

Fortune Cookies

3 egg whites
3/4 c. sugar
1/8 tsp. salt
1/2 c. butter, melted
1/4 tsp. vanilla extract
1 c. flour
1 tbsp. instant tea powder
2 tbsp. water

Preheat the oven to 350°F.

Type or write the fortunes on paper so that when they are cut the pieces will be no larger than 2 inches long and 1/2 inch wide.

Combine the ingredients in the order listed, mixing well after each addition. Chill for 20 minutes.

Make the cookies 2 at a time. On a greased cookie sheet, drop a spoonful of dough for each cookie. Using the back of a spoon, spread the dough very thin, making a 3-inch circle.

Bake 5 minutes, or until the edges are lightly browned. Working quickly, place a paper fortune in the center of each cookie. Fold each cookie in half, enclosing the fortunes, to form a semi-circle. Grasp the rounded edges of the semi-circle between the thumb and forefinger of one hand. Place the forefinger of the other hand at the center of the folded edge and push it in, making sure that the solid side of the cookie puffs out.

Place each cookie in a small muffin tin, open edges up, until cookie is set.

Store in an airtight container.

Chocolate Goober Squares

3 sticks butter
1 c. peanut butter
2 c. sugar
2 eggs, beaten
1 tsp. vanilla extract
1/4 tsp. salt
1 tsp. cinnamon
1/4 c. water
3 c. flour
1 1/2 tsp. baking powder
1/2 c. peanuts, chopped
6 oz. semi-sweet chocolate chips

Cream butter, peanut butter, and sugar. Add eggs, vanilla, salt, and cinnamon. Add water. Mix well.

Add flour and baking powder. Mix well.

Stir in peanuts and chocolate chips.

Press into a 14 x 10-inch or larger pan. The larger the pan, the thinner the squares will be.

Bake in 350° F oven for 25–35 minutes, or until firm.

Cool and cut into squares.

Sweet Breads

Sift:
To put dry ingredients, such as flour,
through a sifter or sieve.

Stir:
To mix ingredients with a spoon using a circular motion.

Whip:
To beat rapidly to increase the volume of an ingredient
such as cream or egg whites.

90-Minute Cinnamon Rolls

3 1/4 c. all-purpose flour, divided
1 envelope Fleischmann's Quick Rise
 Instant Yeast
1/4 c. sugar
1/2 tsp. salt
3/4 c. milk
1/4 c. water
1/4 c. margarine
1 egg
1 c. brown sugar, firmly packed
1 tbsp. cinnamon
1/2 c. margarine, softened
1/2 c. raisins, optional

Set aside 1 cup of flour. Mix remaining flour, yeast, sugar, and salt in large bowl. Heat milk, water, and 1/4 cup margarine until hot to touch. Stir hot liquid into dry ingredients. Mix in egg and enough reserve flour to make a soft dough. Turn out on a floured board and knead 5 minutes. Cover dough and let rise 10 minutes.

Mix brown sugar, cinnamon, and 1/2 cup margarine together. Roll dough into 12 x 9-inch rectangle pan. Spread with cinnamon mixture. Sprinkle with raisins.

Roll up from long side, jelly-roll style; pinch to seal the seam. Cut into 12 equal slices with a sharp knife. Place cut side up in large greased muffin cups. Place muffin pan on baking sheet over a shallow pan half-filled with boiling water. Cover dough and let rise 20 minutes.

Bake at 375°F for 20 minutes, or until browned. Remove from muffin cups to cool. Serve warm.

Makes 12 rolls.

Fruit Coffee Cake

1 1/2 c. unbleached sifted flour
1 c. sugar
2 tsp. baking powder
1/4 tsp. baking soda
1/4 tsp. salt
2 eggs
1 c. sour cream
1/2 tsp. vanilla extract
1/4 c. fresh fruit (blueberries or peaches)

Topping:
5 tbsp. sugar
2 tbsp. butter (softened, not melted)
1 tsp. cinnamon

Heat oven to 350°F. Sift flour with sugar, baking powder, soda, and salt.

In separate bowl, beat together eggs, sour cream, and vanilla extract. Add to flour mixture and beat until smooth.

Spread in a greased 9 x 9-inch baking pan. Dot with fresh fruit.

Mix topping ingredients together until mixture resembles cornmeal.

Sprinkle over batter. Bake for 20–25 minutes, or until toothpick inserted in center comes out clean.

Cinnamon Bread

2 pkgs. yeast
1/2 c. warm water
1 1/2 c. milk, scalded and cooled to lukewarm
2/3 c. vegetable oil
1/2 c. sugar
2 tsp. salt
2 eggs
1 1/2 c. quick cooking oats
5 1/2 c. flour

Filling:
3 tbsp. butter, melted
1 c. sugar
1/4 c. cinnamon

In a large bowl, dissolve yeast in warm water. Add milk, oil, sugar, salt, eggs, and oats. Stir in enough flour to make a stiff dough.

Remove from bowl and knead on a floured surface until dough is satiny and smooth, about 10 minutes. Place in a greased bowl, turning to coat entire ball. Cover and let rise until doubled in size. Punch down and divide into three equal parts. Combine filling ingredients. Roll dough into rectangles and spread each with one-third of filling mixture. Roll up to form a loaf. Seal ends and place seam side down in greased loaf pans.

Cover and let rise for about 1 hour, or until doubled in bulk. Bake at 375°F for about 1 hour, or until golden brown.

Pumpkin Bread

3 c. sugar
1 c. oil
1 can pumpkin
4 eggs, slightly beaten
3 1/2 c. all-purpose flour
2 tsp. baking soda
2 tsp. salt
1 tsp. baking powder
1 tsp. nutmeg
1 tsp. allspice
1 tsp. cinnamon
1/2 tsp. ground cloves
2/3 c. water

Preheat oven to 350°F.

In a large bowl, mix sugar and oil. Add pumpkin and eggs. Blend well. Then, add flour, soda, salt, baking powder, spices, and water. Mix completely. Pour into two, well-greased loaf pans. Bake for 1 to 1 1/2 hours. Bread is done when top springs back when lightly touched.

Zucchini Bread

3 c. grated zucchini
1 c. oil
1 1/2 c. sugar
3 eggs, beaten
1 tsp. vanilla extract
3 c. flour
1 1/2 tsp. baking powder
1 tsp. baking soda
1 1/2 tsp. cinnamon
1 tsp. salt
1/2 tsp. ginger
1 c. chopped nuts
1 c. raisins

Combine zucchini, oil, sugar, eggs, and vanilla extract. In separate bowl, sift together flour, baking powder, baking soda, cinnamon, salt, and ginger. Combine both bowls and stir to blend. Add nuts and raisins and beat 4 minutes. Place in greased loaf pan and bake at 350°F for 1 hour. (This recipe also freezes well.)

Banana Bread

1/2 c. shortening
1 c. sugar
2 eggs
3/4 c. mashed, very ripe banana
1 tsp. vanilla extract
1 1/4 c. sifted flour
3/4 tsp. baking soda
1/2 tsp. salt
1/2 cup chopped nuts (optional)

Cream shortening and sugar until fluffy. Add eggs, one at a time, beating well after each addition. Stir in banana and vanilla extract. Sift dry ingredients together and add to banana mixture. Mix well. Fold in nuts, if desired. Pour into greased loaf pan or 9 x 9 x 2-inch pan. Bake at 350°F for 30–35 minutes.

Apple Coffee Cake

1/2 c. butter
1 1/2 c. sugar
2 eggs
1 c. milk
3 c. all-purpose flour
1 tsp. salt
3 tsp. baking powder
3 apples chopped into 1/2-inch chunks
Crumb Mixture (recipe follows)

Cream butter and sugar together. Add eggs and milk. Sift flour, salt, and baking powder together. Stir into creamed mixture. Stir in half of apple chunks. Pour batter into greased 9 x 13-inch pan. Top with remaining apples chunks. Sprinkle Crumb Mixture evenly over top. Bake at 350°F for about 30 minutes.

Crumb Mixture:

1/2 c. flour
1/2 c. sugar
1 tsp. cinnamon
dash nutmeg
1/4 c. butter

Mix flour, sugar, cinnamon, and nutmeg together. Cut in butter until crumbly.

Strawberry-Pecan Bread

3 c. all-purpose flour
1 tsp. salt
2 c. sugar
1 tsp. baking soda
1 tsp. cinnamon
4 eggs, beaten
1 1/4 c. vegetable oil
2 c. sliced strawberries
1 1/4 c. chopped pecans

Combine the flour, salt, sugar, baking soda, and cinnamon. Add the eggs, oil, strawberries, and pecans. Stir until just moistened.

Spoon the batter into 2 well-greased 9 x 5 x 3-inch loaf pans. Bake at 350°F for 60–70 minutes, or until a toothpick inserted in the center comes out clean.

Cool in the pan for 5 minutes. Remove from pan and cool completely on wire racks.

Blueberry Loaf Cake

2/3 c. blueberries (fresh or frozen)
1 1/2 c. all-purpose flour, divided
1/3 c. yellow cornmeal
1 1/2 tsp. baking powder
1/2 c. plus 1 tbsp. nonfat yogurt
1 tbsp. fresh lemon juice
2/3 c. plus 2 tsp. sugar, divided
1/4 c. vegetable oil
1 tsp. grated lemon zest
1 large whole egg
1 egg white
1/4 tsp. ground cinnamon

Preheat oven to 350°F and place rack in center of oven. Lightly oil an 8 x 4-inch loaf pan and set aside.

Toss blueberries with 1 tablespoon of flour and set aside.

In a small bowl, stir together remaining flour, cornmeal, and baking powder. In another small bowl, combine yogurt and lemon juice.

In a medium bowl, whisk together 2/3 cup of sugar, oil, and lemon zest. Beat in whole egg, then egg white, beating well after each addition. Alternately add the dry ingredients and the yogurt mixture, beginning and ending with the dry ingredients.

Mix until just combined. Gently fold in blueberries. Spoon batter into the prepared pan.

In a small bowl, combine the remaining 2 teaspoons of sugar and cinnamon; sprinkle over the batter.

Bake for 50–60 minutes, or until cake is golden and a toothpick inserted in the center comes out clean. After 25 minutes of baking, cover the pan loosely with aluminum foil. Cool the cake in the pan on a rack for 10 minutes, then turn out on rack and cool completely. For best flavor, wrap the cake and store overnight before serving.

Rich and Famous Shortbread

Crust:
3/4 c. flour
1/4 c. sugar
1/4 c. butter

Caramel Layer:
1/2 c. butter
2 tbsp. corn syrup
1 can (14 oz.) sweetened condensed milk
1 tsp. vanilla extract
1/2 c. semi-sweet chocolate chips

Preheat oven to 350°F.

For the crust, mix the flour, sugar, and butter until crumbly. Press into a greased, 8-inch square pan. Bake for 10–15 minutes, or until golden brown. Set aside to cool.

For the caramel layer, melt the butter in a heavy saucepan. Add the corn syrup and condensed milk. Bring the mixture to a boil. Cook for 12–15 minutes, stirring constantly, until the mixture turns a medium caramel color. Be careful not to let the mixture burn.

Remove from heat and stir in the vanilla extract. Pour the mixture over the prepared crust and allow it to cool. Melt the chocolate chips and spread them over the caramel layer. Cool until set. Cut into bars.

Friendship Cake or Bread

The Friendship Cake Starter:

2/3 c. sugar
2/3 c. milk
2/3 c. flour
2 c. sugar
2 c. flour
2 c. milk

Mix 2/3 cup each of sugar, milk, and flour in a plastic or glass container with a tight lid. Cover and store at room temperature for 17 days, stirring once a day.

After that, leave undisturbed for 1 day. Stir again daily for 3 days. Add 1 cup each of sugar, milk, and flour, then stir daily the next 4 days. Add another cup each of sugar, milk, and flour. Mix well.

Give 1 cup each to 2 friends with the following recipe and use 1 cup to make your own Friendship Cake.

The Friendship Cake:

1 c. Friendship Cake Starter
2/3 c. oil
3 eggs
2 c. flour
1 c. sugar
2 tsp. vanilla extract
2 c. chopped apples
1 1/2 tsp. cinnamon
2 tsp. baking powder
1 1/2 tsp. baking soda
1/2 tsp. salt
1/2 to 1 c. nuts

Combine all ingredients until well mixed. Grease and flour a Bundt or loaf pan. Pour batter into pan and bake in preheated 350°F oven 40–50 minutes. Cool in pan for 10 minutes, then turn out and continue cooling.

Baklava

1 lb. filo dough
1/2 lb. sweet butter
2 c. ground pistachios

Preheat oven to 275°F. Melt butter. Grease 11 x 16-inch jelly roll pan. Lay 1 sheet of filo on bottom of pan and brush with butter. Repeat until you have used half the sheets. Spread nuts evenly over entire surface. Continue layering sheets of filo on top of nut layer. Pour any remaining butter over top. Cut into diagonal strips to form diamond shapes. Bake 2 to 2 1/2 hours, until golden brown on top.

Syrup:

3 c. sugar
2 c. apricot nectar
2 tbsp. honey
1 tbsp. lemon juice

Mix ingredients and bring to a boil. Reduce heat and simmer to a heavy syrup, approximately 20–25 minutes. When baklava is done, drain any excess butter from pastry. Brush surface lightly with butter. Pour warm syrup over pastry a little at a time until all is absorbed. Allow to cool several hours. Makes approximately 30 diamonds.

Nan Nan's Gingerbread

2 eggs, beaten
3/4 c. brown sugar
1 tsp. allspice
3/4 c. molasses
3/4 c. shortening, melted
2 1/2 c. flour
2 tsp. baking soda
1/2 tsp. baking powder
3 tsp. ginger
3 tsp. cinnamon
1/2 tsp. cloves
1 tsp. nutmeg
2 tsp. pumpkin pie spice
1 c. boiling water

Add beaten eggs to sugar, molasses, and melted shortening. Sift dry ingredients and add to egg mixture. Lastly, add boiling water and mix well. Pour into greased and floured Bundt pan. Bake at 350°F for 30–40 minutes.

Easy Caramel Pecan Rolls

5 tbsp. butter
3/4 c. brown sugar
1/4 c. water
1/2 c. chopped pecans
3 tbsp. butter, softened
1/4 c. granulated sugar
2 tsp. cinnamon
2 cans (8 oz. each) crescent rolls

Preheat the oven to 375°F. In a 13 x 9-inch baking pan, melt the 5 tablespoons butter. Stir in the brown sugar, water, and pecans. Separate each can of rolls into 4 triangles and seal the perforations. Spread each with softened butter.

Combine the granulated sugar and cinnamon. Sprinkle the mixture over the buttered dough. Roll up each triangle from the short side. Cut each roll into 4 slices (chill first for easier slicing).

Place the slices in the prepared pan, cut side down. Bake for 20–25 minutes. Immediately turn the rolls over and spoon the remaining sauce over the rolls.

Sour Cream Coffee Cake

3 tbsp. butter, softened
1/3 c. chopped pecans
1/2 c. brown sugar
1 tsp. vanilla extract
3/4 c. granulated sugar
1/2 c. oil
3 eggs
2 c. flour
1 tsp. baking powder
1 tsp. baking soda
1/4 tsp. salt
1 c. sour cream

In a bowl, stir together the butter, pecans, and brown sugar until crumbly; set aside. In a separate bowl, combine the vanilla extract, granulated sugar, oil, and eggs. Beat with an electric mixer until smooth. Sift together the flour, baking powder, baking soda, and salt. Add this mixture to the egg mixture alternately with the sour cream. Mix well after each addition.

Pour half of the batter into a greased tube pan. Layer half of the crumb mixture over this. Pour the remaining batter over the crumbs. Top with the remaining crumb mixture. Bake at 350°F for 50 minutes, or until done.

Notes

Notes

Index